IN CELEBRATION

A miner and his wife are celebrating their fortieth wedding anniversary with their three grown-up sons. During the course of the brothers' conversation, the ostensibly happily married couple are revealed to have been harbouring a secret guilt for which the father feels he has never atoned and for which the sons feel that they have been made to suffer unjustly. The eldest son, Andrew, forces the issue out into the open with his brothers and nearly succeeds with his mother and father. A timely interruption by a neighbour, however, saves them from the confrontation and dooms their Father to his habitual feelings of repressed guilt.

5m 2f

THE HEREFORD PLAYS
General Editor: E. R. Wood

Maxwell Anderson
Winterset

Robert Ardrey
Thunder Rock

Robert Bolt
A Man for All Seasons
The Tiger and the Horse

Harold Brighouse
Hobson's Choice

Coxe and Chapman
Billy Budd

Gordon Daviot
Dickon

Barry England
Conduct Unbecoming

J. E. Flecker
Hassan

Ruth and Augustus
Goetz
The Heiress

H. Granville-Barker
The Voysey Inheritance

(Ed.) E. Haddon
Three Dramatic Legends

Willis Hall
*The Long and the Short
and the Tall*

Fritz Hochwälder
The Strong are Lonely

Henrik Ibsen
The Master Builder
An Enemy of the People

D. H. Lawrence
*The Widowing of Mrs
Holroyd* and *The
Daughter-in-Law*

Roger MacDougall
Escapade

Arthur Miller
The Crucible
Death of a Salesman
All My Sons

Bill Naughton
*Spring and Port
Wine*

André Obey
Noah

J. B. Priestley
An Inspector Calls
Time and the Conways
When We are Married

James Saunders
*Next Time I'll Sing to
You*
A Scent of Flowers

R. C. Sherriff
Journey's End

J. M. Synge
*The Playboy of the West-
ern World* and *Riders
to the Sea*

David Storey
In Celebration

Brandon Thomas
Charley's Aunt

Peter Ustinov
Romanoff and Juliet

John Whiting
Marching Song
Saint's Day
A Penny for a Song
The Devils

Oscar Wilde
*The Importance of Being
Earnest*

Tennessee Williams
The Glass Menagerie

David Storey

In Celebration

with an Introduction by
RONALD HAYMAN

HEINEMANN EDUCATIONAL BOOKS
LONDON

Heinemann Educational Books Ltd
22 Bedford Square, London WC1B 3HH

LONDON EDINBURGH MELBOURNE AUCKLAND TORONTO
HONG KONG SINGAPORE KUALA LUMPUR
IBADAN NAIROBI JOHANNESBURG
NEW DELHI

ISBN 0 435 22835 8

First published by Jonathan Cape Ltd 1969
© 1969 by David Storey
First published in Hereford Plays
Series 1973
Introduction © Ronald Hayman 1973
Reprinted 1977, 1982

Printed in Great Britain by
Spottiswoode Ballantyne Ltd., Colchester and London

Contents

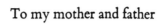

To my mother and father

This play was first presented at the Royal Court Theatre, London, on April 22nd, 1969, under the direction of Lindsay Anderson. The cast was as follows:

Mr Shaw	BILL OWEN
Mrs Shaw	CONSTANCE CHAPMAN
Andrew	ALAN BATES
Colin	JAMES BOLAM
Steven	BRIAN COX
Mrs Burnett	GABRIELLE DAYE
Reardon	FULTON MACKAY

CHARACTERS

MR SHAW, a miner, aged 64
MRS SHAW, his wife, aged 60
ANDREW, aged 38 ⎫
COLIN,   aged 36 ⎬ their sons
STEVEN, aged 33 ⎭
MRS BURNETT, a neighbour, aged 60
REARDON, a neighbour, aged 68

INTRODUCTION

David Storey, the third son of a Yorkshire miner, was born in 1933. He was educated locally, in Wakefield, and after signing on as a professional rugby league footballer at the age of eighteen won a scholarship to study art at the Slade School in London. His life at that period was divided into two – between playing professional rugby in Leeds on Saturdays and painting in London during the week – and he says he found it hard to 'see any connection between the reality of the one thing, a rough and hard game, played for money, and the reality of the other, a completely introverted event calling on, as I then thought, great powers of self-absorption'. He started to write a novel about a man whose life was divided in the same sort of way, but who was more successful in achieving a balance between the two halves, the one derived from the working-class community in which he grew up, and the other from painting. Both miners and professional rugby players tend to be suspicious of artists, if not actually hostile. Why should anyone be allowed to spend his life at home, trying to paint, instead of going out to do a man's job like anyone else?

After leaving the Slade, Storey forfeited a proportion of his signing-on fee and, gaining his release from professional rugby, became a schoolteacher in the East End. By now writing occupied as much of his time as painting. He worked at it with great persistence but without success. Amongst the seven novels he had written and which had been rejected by publishers was one called *This Sporting Life*: it was after eight publishers had turned it down that he decided to try his hand at writing a play. During a half-term he wrote one in three days about a schoolteacher who went mad. He called it *To Die with the Philistines*. He did nothing further with it, but two years later, in 1960, after being rejected altogether fifteen times, his novel *This Sporting Life* was finally published. Both this novel and the one which followed it, *Flight into Camden*, won important prizes. *This Sporting Life* won the American Macmillan Fiction Award, and *Flight into Camden* won both the John Llewellyn Rhys Memorial Prize and the Somerset Maugham Award.

Lindsay Anderson was invited to make a film of *This Sporting Life* and Storey himself was asked to write the screenplay. It was while they were working together that Anderson asked him whether he had ever written or thought of writing for the theatre. He got out his play, did some revision and changed the title to *The Restoration of Arnold Middleton*. Plans were made for the play to be done in 1961 at the Royal Court, and the possibility came up again in 1964, but the first production it actually had was in 1966, at the Edinburgh Traverse Theatre. The following year it got another production at the Royal Court, which transferred to the West End. The play won an Evening Standard Drama Award for 1967.

The experience of seeing three-dimensional performances of a play he had written made Storey want to go on writing for the theatre, a feeling that immediately triggered an extremely productive period in which he turned out six or seven plays in rapid succession, all written very quickly. None of them were staged immediately but by the end of 1971 four of them had been produced by Lindsay Anderson at the Royal Court – *In Celebration* (1969), *The Contractor* (1969), *Home* (1970) and *The Changing Room* (1971).

Of all these plays *In Celebration* is the only one which deals directly with a family background like the one in which Storey himself grew up. The father in *In Celebration* is a coal-miner; one of his three sons has thrown over a legal career to work as a painter; another, a schoolteacher, has tried to write a book and then given it up; the third is a works liaison officer in a car

2

factory. The celebration on which the play hinges is the fortieth wedding anniversary of the miner and his wife. It is this which brings the three sons back into the house they grew up in. We do not actually see the celebration itself, a dinner at a restaurant which takes place during the interval, but the rhythm of the play is determined by the way in which the family reunion briefly interrupts the quiet rhythm of the parents' lives. The play starts as the youngest of the three sons arrives, and it ends on the morning after the party, as all three sons go away again, leaving the old couple with their routine unchanged after the tensions and revelations of the stormy conversations – conversations which have shown how all three sons have been deeply damaged by their family upbringing, or at least how they feel they have. For one of the underlying elements of the play is the juxtaposition of the apparently enlightened views of the liberated sons with the simple suffering humanism of the parents. The father, too, is seen as a victim – not only of the family but of society. He has spent forty-nine of his sixty-four years down the pits, mostly working in a very narrow seam.

> Thirteen inches. If I as much as cough, the whole damn roof'll come down on top of me. Two hundred yards of rock above, and the centre of the earth beneath. Why, you're nothing but a piece of stone yourself, propped up between one bit and the next. You lie with your belly shoved up against your throat.

He has a hacking cough and last week he nearly lost his hand – had to have seven stitches in it.

The mother feels she has married beneath her, and her resentment, both conscious and unconscious, has helped to poison the air that the growing boys breathed. Her first child, Jamey, died, apparently of pneumonia, about three months before Steven was born, and the play suggests that the amount of corporal punishment he received may have weakened his constitution. Andrew, the eldest of the three survivors, seems to have sustained severe psychological damage as a result of being boarded out with a neighbour, a man called Reardon, while his mother, who had been suicidal after the death of her firstborn, had to cope with a new baby.

Andrew, Colin and Steven have all been crippled emotionally by having to grow up in this environment, and their function as characters in the play is to represent three different attitudes to the past and three different ways of surviving it. In terms of earning power, the most successful is Colin, who is the only one that has not settled down into family life himself. His job in the motor industry, negotiating between management and labour, has brought him worldly success but at the cost of his integrity. Of the three men, now all in their thirties, he is the least capable of sincerity. He is also the least likable and the least interested in facing up to the truth about the family's past. His aim is to survive in his private life, as in his career, by compromising cheerfully and papering over his cracks.

Andrew, the central character in the play, is temperamentally at the opposite extreme – a man willing to cause pain rather than conceal the truth. He even takes a certain perverse pleasure in rubbing the salt into emotional wounds, both his own and other people's. The basic facts of human and social existence seem almost intolerable to him.

> ANDREW: Whenever I meet a man who describes himself as a humanist, a rationalist, a man of reason, something in my soul, something deep inside me, calls out – in pain, in protest. 'This man', it tells me, 'is obscene.'
>
> COLIN (*coming in drying face*): It seems there's an awful lot of obscenity in your life, Andy.
>
> ANDREW (*to* STEVEN): When you see a cancer it's no commendation of your powers of loving to fall on your knees and give it a damn great kiss.

His main function in the play is to insist on uncovering unpleasant realities, forcing the others to acknowledge the truth about the past and the effects it has had on the present. For a great deal of Act One it looks as though the dynamic of the play is carrying it towards a big showdown between him and his mother, but the confrontation is avoided. As David Storey has said in an interview:*

In a way the explosion has already taken place, off or outside or away, and this is really the aftermath of the battle. If you compare it with Ibsen in terms of approaching emotional realities, Ibsen is writing about what happened before the explosion: the bomb is festering away inside, and it does go off. *In Celebration* is after the bomb's shown what it can do. The aftermath of revelation is only too obvious. It's not a question of stripping off hypocrisies and deceits and complacencies, but of realizing that once you have there is nothing there afterwards.

I would have said that it could only have been written fifty or a hundred years after Ibsen in that sense. There really is no stripping away any more. All the illusions in that sense have gone. People may stick to the lying. The bomb is there and we no longer need the explosion, the ripping out of heart and head. It really is a question of soldiering on or of compromise or forgiveness, as the play tentatively suggests at the end. I don't know if this is a kind of author's self-indulgence or not. If it is then the play is a failure, because I have so strongly implanted in me the belief that if it doesn't work, then there really isn't that much play there.

I think *The Contractor*'s a similar case of a deliberate withdrawal from drama in that sense. Again all the confrontations that could take place are, if you like, skilfully avoided, because the actual conception of the play is directed towards that end rather than explosion and revelation.

Andrew is the only character in *In Celebration* who could have provoked the explosion. Steven is not one to paper over cracks but he is by nature a silent sufferer. The play's suggestion is that he is still, in some sense, inside the womb, waiting to be born. The book he started to write had been putting forward a view

* In *Drama*, Spring 1971.

of society with which Andrew was in agreement, but Steven was unable to finish it. He cannot exteriorize his sufferings. He cries in his sleep but cannot explain, cannot excuse.

> I look as sick as I do – if I do look sick – because I'm not a moralist like you. In the end, attitudes like you've described are easily adopted. All you have to do is throw over what's already there. You're like an evangelist. You both are. You forget there's another kind of temperament.

This temperament seems very similar to the temperament Jamey had. Andrew remembers him:

> I was nearly five. I remember him very well. Sitting there . . . drawing. . . . Or upstairs. Crying. They never beat us you know. But him . . . he was black and blue. . . . And like Steven there – but for his little bloody pictures – *silent as the tomb.*

Apart from the parents and the three sons, the only other characters in the play are the two neighbours, Mrs Burnett and Mr Reardon, who are both, like the parents, in their sixties. Life for the old folk is very much the same as it was thirty years ago, with the one difference that they have now used up most of their time. Mrs Burnett is very much the conventional neighbour – kind-hearted, mindless, lonely, insatiable in her thirst for gossip and her thirst for tea. Reardon is much more interesting. The main pleasure left to him is to drink, but with him, as with the three sons, there is a strong sense of intellectual ability gone to waste. He now talks with the same cynicism about his work and about his apocalyptic vision.

> Certain irregularities in the local office of the National Coal Board have allowed me to spend rather longer than I legally am entitled to in the colliery office, checking pay, attempting, in my own small way, to settle amicably the various disputes – soothing the manager's sorrow, the deputy's rage, appeasing whenever I could the miner's consternation . . . I have seen two world wars and several minor ones,

and not a little of my life's energies have been expended in avoiding each and everyone: I have lived through the most calamitous half-century since time began and my instinct for war, for rivalry and destruction is unparalleled, I would imagine, by almost anyone. I have a vision, Mrs Burnett, a presentiment . . . of a holocaust so gigantic, so monumental in its proportions, that beside it all our little dreams and hopes, our sorrows, and our little aims and fears . . . must count as nothing. Whether these are the sort of visions endemic to a man very close to retiring age – and to a pension it can only humiliate him to receive – or whether they are a definitive view of reality as we and our children shall eventually come to know it – I cannot say. All I can see before me, I must confess, are flames, – flames, pillage, burning, terror.

It can be objected that this element is not integrated into the play's organism. Perhaps what Reardon is talking about is what Steven is keeping silent about. Perhaps this speech, which comes from outside the family and outside the main action, is more autobiographical, more related to David Storey's own inner development than anything else in the play. Certainly it corresponds closely with the vision he articulates in his third published novel *Radcliffe*. The play may not, ultimately, succeed in establishing an organic connection between this vision and the statements it is making. Nor are the two main statements sufficiently related to each other. What exactly is the relationship between the way that society has harmed the father and the way that the family has harmed the sons? But the play does succeed in building up a very considerable atmosphere and tension, and in illuminating – not consistently but with irregular flashes of insight – some of the main pressures on and within working-class life in England today.

ACT ONE

Scene 1

A solid, heavily-furnished living-room: a door on one side leads to the kitchen and the stairs, a door on the other side to the front door and the road. There is also a window and a fireplace. The furniture is heavy and provincial: a three-piece suite, a table and four chairs, and a sideboard. There are various cushions, photographs and pictures, as well as several cowboy paperbacks. The atmosphere is one of sobriety, with no particularly distinguishing features, either of period or 'character'.

Mid-morning. STEVEN *comes in carrying a battered brief-case. He's dressed in an overcoat: a man in his thirties.*

STEVEN. Dad? ... (*Looks round*) Dad?

> (*He hears a sound. Puts his bag down. Rubs his hands against the cold. Wanders round the room, examining old, familiar objects. One or two he picks up, shakes his head, etc.*
> SHAW *comes in from the stairs: small and stocky, he's just woken, and is dressed in trousers and shirt, the shirt unfastened, the trousers held up by braces.*)

Dad ...

SHAW. Steven ... You're early. I've scarcely woken up. (*They shake hands.*)

... What time ... (*Looks round dazedly*) ... I thought you weren't coming till this afternoon.

STEVEN. I got away early ...

SHAW. Aye, well ... How are you? You're looking all right.

> (SHAW *is a bit shy of his son.*)

STEVEN (*taking his coat off*). So's yourself. A bit older ... a bit more weight to go with it.

SHAW. Oh, take no notice of me ... I only got back from work three or four hours ago. Nights. My age ... You'd think they'd give me summat else ... Your mother's out ...

9

STEVEN. Yes ... I met a woman down the road ... she told me ...

SHAW. Nowt they don't know round here ... Gone to buy herself a hat.

STEVEN. A hat ...

SHAW. For tonight. (*Looking round for his cigarettes*) I can't tell you ... I've heard nothing else for the past fortnight. You'd think we'd come up with a few thousand ...

(*Finds his cigarette packet on the mantelpiece: offers one to* STEVEN.)

No, you don't, do you? Common sense. I'm choked up to here ... (*Coughs as he lights his own.*) Coal-dust. It's a wonder I'm still alive.

STEVEN. I've heard that before.

SHAW. Aye. But you won't for much longer.

STEVEN. I've heard that before as well.

SHAW (*sighs*). Aye ... Do you fancy a cup of tea? I'll just make one. (*Going*) How's the family, then? ... Are they keeping well? (*Goes to the kitchen.*)

STEVEN (*talking through*). All right ... Up and down ... Look at this ... I don't think ought's changed here since I was last up ...

SHAW (*reappearing*). Family, lad. Family. There's nothing as important as that. A good wife: children. God's good grace. (*Looks briefly up*) If you have good health and your family, you don't need anything else.

STEVEN. Aye ...

SHAW. Sixty-four years next month. If I haven't learnt that I've learnt nothing. (*Suddenly shows him his hand*) Damn near lost me hand last week. Seven stitches.

STEVEN. You'll have to watch out.

SHAW. Watch out? My age ... You're joking. One more year, you know, then I'm finished. Pension me off. Fifty years, you know, I've been down that lot. That's what I've got to show. (*Holds up his hands.*)

STEVEN. Oh, and a bit more ...

SHAW. Nay, I can't grumble ... And how's your lot? How's Sheila? Best daughter-in-law I ever had.

STEVEN. She's all right.

SHAW. Four kiddies. There can't be ten months between them. I don't know how they do it. I thought I was impetuous. There was two or three years, you know, between you lot.

STEVEN. When are they getting up?

SHAW. I don't know. This afternoon. Colin's bringing Andrew up in his car. They'll get here sometime, I suppose. Your mother hasn't been able to sit down for two minutes. Up and down. You'll have to toss up for who's sleeping where. One down here, two up yonder. It'll be like old times. She's cleaned that floor a dozen times if she's cleaned it once. And them windows ... it's a wonder there's any glass left in. Almost polished them right through ... (*Looks out*) Nothing changed out there either, you can see. Houses ... houses ... houses ... as far as the eye can see ... That's the kettle ... Get your jacket off. Make yourself at home ... Mind where you put yourself. She's puffed up every cushion, straightened every chair. It's like being in the army ... (*He goes out to the kitchen. Off*) How long are you staying?

STEVEN. I'll have to get back tomorrow.

SHAW (*off*). How's your work going?

STEVEN. All right.

SHAW (*popping in the door*). I wish I got half of what you got, I can tell you: and for doing twice as much. I wouldn't mind.

STEVEN. It's got its drawbacks.

SHAW. Drawbacks. It could draw back as far as it liked for me ... Teaching. Good God ... Ay up. Ay up. She's here. Look out. Look out.

(*He goes back in the kitchen.* MRS BURNETT *comes in; a neighbour, in her early sixties.*)

MRS BURNETT. Thought I saw you, Steven ... How are you keeping, love?

STEVEN. Hello, Mrs Burnett … Well enough …

MRS BURNETT. And how's your wife?

STEVEN. Oh, surviving.

MRS BURNETT. I know. I've heard … They've shown me photographs, you know …

SHAW (*off*). Pretend she's not there. She'll go away. Just take no notice.

MRS BURNETT. Doesn't mind me popping in. Always the same … And your kiddies?

STEVEN. Fine.

MRS BURNETT. Your mother never mentions them. But I know. It all goes on inside. She's that sort of woman.

STEVEN. She's out shopping.

MRS BURNETT. I saw her go. New hat. She's very excited about tonight. Where are you taking them?

STEVEN. Into town … Colin's arranged something.

MRS BURNETT. Your Andrew and Colin not here, then, yet?

STEVEN. They're coming up by car.

MRS BURNETT. Eh. It's a lovely treat for them.

STEVEN. I hope so.

MRS BURNETT. Forty years. They'll not forget …

SHAW (*coming with a tray and two pots*). Yakking. Yakking. Yakking.

MRS BURNETT (*to* STEVEN). He never lets you get a word in. Don't worry.

SHAW. Word in? I can hardly open me mouth … (*To* STEVEN) Smells tea, you know, a mile off. The 'uman blood 'ound. She's never out of this house.

MRS BURNETT. He hasn't forgotten me, don't worry, after all these years.

SHAW. No. That's true.

MRS BURNETT. He doesn't let you forget, don't worry. He's out showing it across the backs whenever he has any news. You get tired of hearing it, I can tell you …

SHAW. Tired? They spend all their day flat on their backs round here. They don't know what work is. As soon as their husband's gone off, out it comes: teapot, cushion behind their backs, feet up ...

MRS BURNETT. I know. I know. That's why you never have anything to eat and your houses are full up to the chimney with last week's washing.

SHAW. Last week's. Last bloody year's more likely. (*To* STEVEN) We've to bolt the door you know at times just to get a bit of peace.

MRS BURNETT (*to* STEVEN). Never changes. All the years I've known him ... Last week he gave your mother a shock. (*Looking at* SHAW *concernedly*.) Came in. White as a sheet. He was.

SHAW. Jumping up and down.

MRS BURNETT. They had me fetch the doctor.

SHAW (*to* STEVEN). Heart ... (*Taps his chest*.)

MRS BURNETT (*to* STEVEN). Don't worry. He didn't treat it lightly.

SHAW. 'Better take it easy. More rest.'
I said: 'You must be joking. How would you take it easy if you had a ten ton rock coming down on top of your head?'

STEVEN. What did he say?

SHAW. He laughed. They don't give a damn. Why should they? An old man. It's a wonder I wasn't dead years ago. She'll tell you ...

MRS BURNETT. Go on ...

SHAW. And that's what he thought, an' all. You can see it in his eyes when he examines you.

STEVEN. I don't think that's right, somehow.

SHAW. Nay. I've no illusions. None ... I've had a good life. With a lovely woman. Can't ask for anything more ... Still ...

MRS BURNETT. Aye ... Well ... (*Gazes at* SHAW *fondly*.)

SHAW. Go on. Go on ... Get shut. (*To* STEVEN) Waiting

for a cup of tea. Be here all day if she has the chance.

MRS BURNETT (*to* STEVEN). I'll pop in later, love. Remember ... (*Gesturing at* SHAW *behind his back*) Pinch of salt. (*Goes.*)

HAW. Pinch of bloody salt ... I'll pinch her bloody salt. Noses ten miles long round here ... She'll be out yakking it across the backs.

STEVEN. Aye. (*Laughs.*)

SHAW. We had a letter from Colin the other week. First one I can tell you for some time. He's moved his job. Works' liaison. A factory that big it'd take you a fortnight to walk right round it ... Cars ...

STEVEN. So I heard ...

SHAW. Offered to get us one. Brand new. Cut price.

STEVEN. You ought to take it.

SHAW. Nay, what would I do with a car? If you can't shove it, pedal it, or hang it on a wall, it's no use to me ... He has to argue, you know ...

STEVEN. Yes ...

SHAW. Whenever the workers – that's us – are going on strike, or feel they ought to, Colin's the one the management calls out to negotiate. He can charm the horns off a bloody cow, that lad. Been like it since I've known him. Industrial relations ... When he was lying on that rug I little thought that that's where he'd end up. Industrial relations. A family with relatives like ours, an' all.

STEVEN. Aye ... (*They laugh.*)

SHAW. Offered to buy us a house, you know. Probably will when we retire. If I'm daft enough to let him ...

STEVEN. It sounds like a good idea.

SHAW. If you're used to having money. As it is, I'm used to nowt. Still, times change. And people with it. Told me I ought to get out, you know. Retire now. He'd put up all the cash.

STEVEN. Why don't you?

SHAW. What? ... (*Gets up, wanders round.*) Andrew's another one, you know. Chucked up his job to be an artist! He's only forty, with two children to support, one of them nearly old enough to go to university. It takes some reckoning. A career as a solicitor, that he's worked at ... that *I* worked at. I've spent some hours, you know, working at that table with him: fractions, decimals, Latin ... Do you know I'd go down that pit some nights declining or declensing, I've forgotten which, Latin verbs ... I could have set up as a schoolmaster any time. Greek, algebra, physics, chemistry: the lot. It's a wonder I haven't taken a university degree myself.

STEVEN. I seem to remember ...

SHAW. Nay. You were the last Steve, but by God, the best. There wasn't much I had to teach you. As for them: I had to shove it down their throats. Like trying to eat burnt porridge.

STEVEN. How's Andrew making his money, then?

SHAW. Don't ask me. One of the reasons he's coming up, I shouldn't wonder, is to see if he can borrow a bit. He's never been one to refuse a back-hander: that's why he was so good at law. He could make it fit any set of facts he wanted ... I remember him coming home when he was about thirteen and proving to me that God no longer existed. He's never looked back since then.

STEVEN. Why don't you take up Colin's offer? We could all chip in a bit.

SHAW. Aye, well ... (*Moves away.*)

STEVEN. What difference does one year make?

SHAW. I first went down the pit when I was fifteen, lad.

STEVEN. Yes.

SHAW. Forty-nine years. Half a century. One more now and it'll make it a round number.

STEVEN. Not worth risking your health for.

SHAW. No. Well ... (*Gazes out of the window.*) Do you remember the war? I used to take one of you, out yonder ...

STEVEN. Me.

SHAW. You? I believe it was. They hardly bombed here. Must have flown over and not thought we were worth it.

STEVEN. Made a mistake there.

SHAW. What? They made no mistakes about that. Miles of nothing, this place. Always has been, always will be. The only thing that ever came out of here was coal. And when that's gone, as it will be, there'll be even less. Row after row of empty houses, as far as the eye can see ... It's starting ... I pass them on the way to work. I stop sometimes and look in – holes in the roof, doors gone, windows ... I knew the people who lived there ... All this was moorland a hundred years ago. Sheep. And a bit of wood ... When they come in a thousand years and dig it up they'll wonder what we made such a mess of it for ... (*Gestures at the walls.*) Look at these foundations and think we all lived in little cells. Like goats.

STEVEN. We did (*He laughs, gets up and pours himself some more tea.*)

SHAW. Aye ... Here. Have a drop of something stronger. I got a bit in, in case ...

STEVEN (*looks at the clock*). A bit early.

SHAW. Save it till later. Don't worry. We'll have a grand time tonight. They'll have seen nothing like it round here for years ... (*Watches him*) How's your book going, then?

STEVEN. All right ...

SHAW. If one of them was going to be famous, you know ... I always thought it would be you.

STEVEN. Why's that? (*Laughs.*)

SHAW. Nay. I don't know. I suppose because you were so clever. (*Shy*) Don't tell me it's something you forget ...

STEVEN. I think I must have done.

SHAW. Aye ...

    (STEVEN *glances away, across the room.*)
Here. Do you want a wash? ... I'll forget my own head one of these days.

STEVEN. I'll go up ... Have a look around ...

SHAW. Not much to see ... I can tell you that. Two rooms, back and front. (*Laughs.*)

(STEVEN *goes to the door.*)

If the water's not hot enough, give us a shout and I'll heat some up for you ... Won't take a minute.

STEVEN. Right ...

(*He goes.*

SHAW *looks a little aimlessly about the room: picks up* STEVEN's *overcoat then his brief-case: looks round for somewhere to put them, then puts them down together in a chair. Looks at the fire, puts on a piece of coal, picks up bucket to take outside to fill ... There's the sound of the outer door shutting. He looks up, puts the bucket down quickly, and sits down in a chair.*

MRS SHAW *comes in, dressed from shopping: 60 years old, matronly, circumspect: some authority and composure.*)

MRS SHAW. There you are ... (*Puts her bag on the table.*)

SHAW (*pleasant*). Nay, and where else would I be?

MRS SHAW. Have you had some tea, then? ... (*Looks at the tray on the table.*)

SHAW. Aye ... Aye ...

MRS SHAW. Two of you.

SHAW. Aye ... Mrs Burnett came in.

MRS SHAW. Did she? And you gave her some tea, then? (*Matter-of-fact, taking off her gloves and coat.*)

SHAW. Well, I thought I better ...

MRS SHAW. Oh, yes. And what's going on, then?

SHAW. Going on? ... Oh. Aye ... Steven's here. I forgot.

MRS SHAW. Forgot.

SHAW. Slipped me mind ... He's upstairs. Having a wash.

MRS SHAW. Having ... Did you give him a clean towel?

SHAW. Towel ... I forgot.

MRS SHAW. Honestly ...

SHAW. It's a wonder the entire street didn't tell you.

MRS SHAW. Well, they didn't. I suppose I've got to ask to find out. (*Picks up tray to take out.*)

(*Sounds of* STEVEN *returning.* MRS SHAW *looks quickly round the room.*)

SHAW. Don't worry. Nothing moved. Nothing shifted.

MRS SHAW. We could do with some more coal.

SHAW. Aye ... (*Gets up slowly.*)

(MRS SHAW *has put the tray down again and goes to the curtains, pulling them back slightly, adjusting them needlessly until she knows* STEVEN *is in the room.*)

MRS SHAW. Well, then. And where have you been all this time?

STEVEN. Oh. About ...

(*He comes to her and embraces her, rather shyly.*)

MRS SHAW. You're not looking too good, love.

STEVEN. The climate. I'm not used to it up here.

MRS SHAW. Aren't they looking after you?

STEVEN. They are. All right.

(SHAW *has gone to the bucket, picked it up, watching them, smiling, then goes out.*)

MRS SHAW. Here. Let's have a look at you. You've put on a lot of weight. Or taken a lot off. I can't remember ... (*She laughs.*)

STEVEN. I forget myself.

MRS SHAW. Have you had some tea? I'll get you something to eat ...

STEVEN. There's no hurry ...

MRS SHAW. How's the family?

STEVEN. Oh. Well.

MRS SHAW. They'll need a lot of upkeep. How old's Roger? Three months? Patrick scarcely one and a quarter ...

STEVEN. I don't know. I've lost count.

MRS SHAW. Well, I don't know. There seems to be a lot of them.

(*Collects tray again*) I'll just put this away ... I hope your Dad hasn't been on too much.

STEVEN. No ... We were talking.

MRS SHAW. I think you'd do a lot of good, you know, while you're up there, if you persuaded him to come out of that pit. He's only another year ...

STEVEN. He's told me.

MRS SHAW. Pride. You've never seen anything like it. (*Hears him coming*) I'll just take this out.

SHAW (*coming in with the bucket of coal*). Now, then, my old china ... (*Puts it down in the hearth*) I'm good for lifting if I'm good for nowt else. When I come again I think they'll make me into a donkey. Reincarnation. It's stamped all over me from head to foot ...

STEVEN. You better be careful. Somebody might hear you.

SHAW. Oh, she knows me. Ought to. Well enough.

STEVEN. I meant up there. (*Points up.*)

SHAW. Oh ... He goes His own way. Nothing I say'll alter that. Don't you think she's looking well?

STEVEN. Yes. I think so ...

SHAW. Forty years of married bliss ... It's left its mark. When she walks down that street they step back, you know, to bow to her. If I come back as a donkey she'll come back as a queen.

(MRS SHAW *comes back in.*)

We were just saying, love. You look a picture.

MRS SHAW. I know. And what of?

SHAW. Nay. You don't need me to tell you. She spends that long at the mirror that when I go to look at it I still find her there – looking out.

(STEVEN *laughs.*)

MRS SHAW. He doesn't change, does he? You should see him skip in the back and comb his hair when Mrs Burnett comes around.

SHAW. Mrs Burnett? I'd need to be down to the last woman on

earth to consider that ... As it is, love, I'm still up with the first. (*Puts his arm round her shoulder, kissing her cheek: she moves her head back slightly and moves away.*)

MRS SHAW. I tell you. He hasn't known where to put himself since he's known you were coming ... I don't think, ever since you went to university, he's known what to do with himself. And that's how long ago?

SHAW. Fifteen years.

STEVEN. Longer ...

SHAW. Education lad: you can't get anywhere without ... Look at your mother. She left school at sixteen. Sixteen. That was almost retiring age in those days. She's still got her certificate upstairs ...

STEVEN. I remember ...

SHAW. 'Proficiency in Domestic Science, Nature Study, and the English Language.' All done out in copperplate script. 'Miss Helen Swanson.' Her father was a pig-breeder, you know. Just outside town.

MRS SHAW. A small-holder ...

SHAW. A pig-breeder! He kept pigs. By go, you had to be in love to step in that house, I can tell you. (*He laughs.*)

MRS SHAW. Well. I've heard some things ...

SHAW. And she ends up marrying me. Never forgiven me, have you, love? ... Nay, lass, you know I love you. I married you all the same. (*He laughs and kisses her cheek.*)

MRS SHAW (*stepping back*). I'll see about some food. (*To* STEVEN) Colin and Andrew are driving up together. They won't get here until this afternoon. I'll show you my hat later, love.

STEVEN. Ah ... Yes.

SHAW. Won't frighten us all, then, will it? Remember, we've got to walk down that street beside you. In public. I don't mind being seen with a woman ...

MRS SHAW. Well, then, in that case you needn't be ashamed.

SHAW. Ashamed? I've never been ashamed, love. Whatever you

wear, my darling, I've never been – and I never will be – ashamed.

MRS SHAW. Well, then, in that case, we'll be all right.

(*She goes, smiling at* STEVEN.)

SHAW (*to* STEVEN). Embarrassed, now. I might be a bit embarrassed. But I wouldn't be ashamed.

(*They laugh.*)

She's a good woman. A lady ... One of the very best. You know, no one's ever got the better of her.

STEVEN. I can imagine.

SHAW. Bit of a let-down, marrying me.

STEVEN. Oh, now. I wouldn't have thought so.

SHAW. Nay, lad. Never one to grumble ... (*Brightly*) Well, then ... What's it like to be back home, Steve?

STEVEN. Home ...

SHAW. After all this time.

STEVEN. Well, I don't know, Dad ... Very much the same.

(*They laugh.*)

FADE

Scene 2

Afternoon. MRS SHAW *is straightening the room, putting chairs more certainly in their places, straightening ornaments, mirror, pictures.*

There's a knock, then a banging on the outside door: whistles, etc.

MRS SHAW. Oh ... (*Looks at herself in the mirror, goes off to the kitchen. Bolts are drawn, locks turned*)

(*Off*) Andrew ... There you are, then, love ...

ANDREW (*off*). Been whistling half an hour ... (*Sounds of embrace*) On the lav, then, were you?

MRS SHAW (*off*). I was not!

ANDREW (*off*). By go ... There's a lot been put on round here ...

MRS SHAW (*off*). Get on. Go on ...

(ANDREW *enters: a fierce, compelling-looking figure dressed in a fairly dishevelled raincoat.*)

ANDREW. Where is he? Where's he hiding? (*Calls*) I'll be up there, old lad! (*To* MRS SHAW) Snoring off his head ... I'll go up and tip him out ...

MRS SHAW. You won't ...

ANDREW. What ... ?

MRS SHAW. He's out ... Went down to the pub. With Steven ...

ANDREW. Steven ...

MRS SHAW. After dinner ... I've been expecting them any minute ... Isn't Colin with you, then?

ANDREW. He's coming on behind. Don't worry ... (*Going round, inspecting room*) Steven's here, then, is he? Might have known ... First in. Last out.

MRS SHAW. Go on. Get on ...

ANDREW. Like a museum is this. Hasn't changed in five thousand years.

MRS SHAW. We've just had it decorated. A few months ago.

ANDREW. What with, then ... soot? (*Runs his hand over the wall.*)

MRS SHAW. I can see somebody hasn't changed. I can.

ANDREW (*picks up paperback*). *Battle at Bloodstone Creek.* I used to marvel at that. My dad's reading age hasn't risen beyond when he was ten years old.

MRS SHAW. We can't all be educated, you know.

ANDREW. No. No. Thank God for that.

MRS SHAW. Where is Colin, anyway?

ANDREW. Parking his car. Got moved on by a policeman.

MRS SHAW. Not here?

ANDREW. No. No. In town. Never seen anything like it. Bigger than a bus. Antagonized them, I believe, no end. Dropped off to buy a packet of cigarettes. 'Can't park that here.' ... Police.

MRS SHAW. Police ...

ANDREW. Got to watch my step ... These days in particular.

MRS SHAW. I thought you were a lawyer.

ANDREW. Was, my dear. Was. Am no longer.

MRS SHAW. I don't know what Peggy thinks. She must be out of her mind, worrying. What are you living on?

ANDREW. On love, my dear. Love. Like everybody else. We've been married now, you know, for seventeen years. If we haven't got a bit of that in stock then we might as well not try.

MRS SHAW (*glances out*). I've heard of living on love before. With Steven. Going to be a writer. And now look at him: four kiddies in as many years, and he looks older than any of you.

ANDREW. Ah well. Steven always was a difficult boy. An infant prodigy, if I remember rightly. What we did under duress he did by nature ...

MRS SHAW. At school they said they'd never seen anything like it. (ANDREW *looks across at her: she's gone to the window again, glancing out.*)
Where is he, then? It's not outside.

ANDREW. End of the road. Gone to find a garage. Didn't want to risk it: leaving it outside.

MRS SHAW. I'm not surprised ... Nowadays ... I don't know ... (*Comes back*) How are you living? ... What sort of pictures do you paint?

ANDREW. I know ... (*Prompting her, goading.*)

MRS SHAW. What ... ?

ANDREW. You think I paint young ladies.

MRS SHAW. What? (*Retreats.*)

ANDREW. Or better still – young men.

MRS SHAW. What ... ?

ANDREW (*pursuing her*). Come on. Admit it ... You think I'm painting young ladies with no clothes on ... She thinks I gave up my career as one of the greatest solicitors in the land in order to peruse certain ladies without their clothes on.

MRS SHAW. I thought nothing of the sort.

ANDREW. Come on. Come on. (*Stalking her round the furniture*) You're as bad as Peggy. She thought the same.

MRS SHAW. I'm not surprised.

ANDREW. You see. I'm right ... Just see what it is I'm up against ... I really puzzled her.

MRS SHAW. What?

ANDREW. Puzzled. Abstract. Not a sign of human life.

MRS SHAW. What ... ? (*Looking around.*)

ANDREW. Me picture ... Peggy ... Came home from me studio with it tucked underneath my arm. Thought she was going to see ... Well, I don't know what she thought she was going to see. She was half-blushing before I'd even put it down. She knew, you see, I'd had me eye on the wife of the chap, from whom I rent my studio, for some considerable time ... but ... lo and behold. Triangles.

MRS SHAW. Triangles?

ANDREW. Or very nearly. The fact is, I'm not very good ... Subtle indentations on either side. Bit here ... Bit there ... Each one a different colour ... the variations in which would almost deceive the eye ... beautiful. If you like triangles, that is ... Abstract.

MRS SHAW. Abstract?

ANDREW. Not a sign of human life.

MRS SHAW. Oh.

ANDREW. Just the first. After that: squares.

MRS SHAW. Squares ...

ANDREW. Rectangles. *Rhomboids*. Sometimes, even – nothing.

MRS SHAW. Nothing?

ANDREW. Well, I say nothing ... there'd be a little ... spot ... of something, here and there. A little red ... (*Paints it for her*) ... cerulean ... touch of viridian ... trickle here ... lovely. Still ... old-fashioned.

MRS SHAW. Old-fashioned?

ANDREW. Absolutely. Don't use paint now, you know.

MRS SHAW. Oh, well ... (*Dismissing it, turning away.*)

ANDREW. Plastic compounds. Plus: miscellaneous bric-à-brac picked up from the refuse dump outside the town. Got arrested once. Loitering with intent. Rang rings round them at the station. 'You better get a solicitor,' they said. 'I am a solicitor,' I said. 'Why, Mr Shaw,' they said, 'we didn't recognize you.' 'Artist now, mate,' I said. 'Don't you forget it.'

MRS SHAW. I can't understand why you gave it up. After all the years you spent studying. It seems a terrible waste. You were never interested in art before.

ANDREW. No ... I'm not now, either.

MRS SHAW. Well, then ... It's not as if you were independent. There's Peter and Jack. It'll be years before they're financially independent.

ANDREW. I don't know so much. I'm thinking of sending them out to support me. I don't think, paradoxical as it may seem, Mother, that I can, any longer, afford to educate my children.

MRS SHAW. Well ... I ... (*Gestures about her.*)

ANDREW. What is it?

MRS SHAW. I've said enough. You must know what you're doing. (*Goes to window again.*)

ANDREW (*Picks up another paperback*). *Phoenix Showdown*. He must get through these faster than he does a cigarette.

MRS SHAW. He brings them home from work. I don't know where he gets them from.

ANDREW. I hope you fumigate them before they come into the house?

MRS SHAW. Well. I've thought about it a time or two, I can tell you.

ANDREW. I bet. I bet ... No alien bodies in this house. That's always been our motto ... What was that subject ... ?

MRS SHAW. Subject?

ANDREW. You were always top in at school.

MRS SHAW. Domestic science.

ANDREW. No ... no ...

MRS SHAW. Human hygiene.

ANDREW. Human hygiene ... I remember you telling us when
we were lads ... human hygiene ... the sort of vision those
words created ...

MRS SHAW. It was an experimental class ... It was the first time it
was ever taught in a school ...

ANDREW. And never looked back since ... No wonder we were
so clean ... Came top, eh?

MRS SHAW. Well ...

ANDREW. Used to tell me friends about it at school ... human
hygiene ... frightened them all to death. They thought ...
well, I don't know what they thought ... Anyway. Never had
any trouble with them after that.
    (*They laugh.*)

MRS SHAW (*looking out*). Now, look ... There he is. You see ...
he must have walked for miles ... I don't know. (*She goes
to the kitchen.* ANDREW *picks up another book, drops it, looks
round.*)

COLIN (*calls*). Hello ... ? (*Comes in the other door: a professional
man in his middle thirties, not smooth, firm, a bit rough. He's
dressed in a Crombie overcoat.*)

ANDREW. Hello.

COLIN. What ... ?

ANDREW. I say: 'hello'.

COLIN. Oh ...

ANDREW. She thinks you're coming in the back.

COLIN. Mother ... (*Crossing to the kitchen.*)

ANDREW. Did you park the car?

COLIN. Yes ...

MRS SHAW (*coming in*). There you are! I thought ... (*They
embrace*) Well, love. It's been a long time ...

ANDREW. Trust him to come in the front. Only for royalty is that. Workers, you know, have to use the rear.

MRS SHAW (*to* COLIN). Take no notice of him, Colin. He's in one of his moods.

ANDREW. Iconoclastic.

COLIN. What?

ANDREW. I'm iconoclastic ... I remember her looking it up when I was how old ... eleven or twelve ... 'I've got just the word for you, my lad,' she said, and got out her dictionary ... you know, her first prize for ...

COLIN. Hygiene.

ANDREW. You see! He remembers that ...

MRS SHAW. I don't remember looking ...

ANDREW. I didn't dare mention it for years. I went round, all that time, thinking it was some sort of sexual deviation.

MRS SHAW. Well, I don't remember that.

ANDREW. Iconoclastic ... The first girl I ever went out with. When I took her home and we'd got to her gate, moon-shining, I said, 'I better warn you, before you start anything, I'm iconoclastic.' 'Oh,' she said, 'well, I better go in, then.' 'Yes,' I said, 'I think you should.'

COLIN. Three hours of that I've had in the car. You've heard about his painting?

(ANDREW *has picked up another paperback, reading it, still standing.*)

MRS SHAW. I have.

COLIN. The only reason he took it up was because they couldn't stand his conversation in his office any longer. There was nobody – no clients, no staff, no nothing – to listen to him at all.

MRS SHAW. He's got his father's nature right enough.

ANDREW. I think I must have. (*Indicating book*) I might take a few of these back with me. (*Holds it to* COLIN) *Massacre in Wolf Canyon.*

27

COLIN Where is he, by the way? In bed?

ANDREW. At the pub.

MRS SHAW. He went with Steven for a drink. After lunch.

ANDREW. Lunch. (*Winks at* COLIN) Used to be dinner in my day ...

MRS SHAW (*to* COLIN). Is there anything I can get you?

COLIN. I could do with a cup of tea. I've walked for miles. Did he tell you about being stopped in town? Five minutes: it couldn't have been any longer.

MRS SHAW. I don't know. It makes your blood boil ... I don't know what it's coming to ... I don't. Not any more.

ANDREW. A police state.

COLIN. It is ... I've parked it down at Sugden's. Not safe to leave it parked out here.

MRS SHAW. Here. I'll make some tea, love ... There's your Dad, now. And Steven. I won't be a minute. (*Goes.*)

(*There are sounds of arrival from the kitchen.*)

ANDREW. All right ... ? (*Nods amicably at* COLIN.)

COLIN. All right?

ANDREW. Tie straight ... buttons ... Little over to the left ... Smashing.

(*He straightens* COLIN's *tie, coat, etc.*)

MRS SHAW (*off*). You're back, then.

STEVEN (*off*). In one piece.

SHAW (*off*). Haven't been too long, I hope, my dear? (*Kiss.*)

MRS SHAW (*off*). Colin and Andrew are here.

SHAW (*off*). Are they? Are they? So we heard. (*Entering*) There you are, then ... Heard about your commotion. How are you, lad? How are you? (*He shakes their hands in turn.*)

COLIN. You're looking pretty well yourself.

ANDREW. Damned old wreck. How many have you had?

SHAW. Ay, now. I go down there for social reasons. Not for anything else.

ANDREW. Aye. We know ...

SHAW. Nay, I'm not the drinker in the house. She's in there, stok-
ing up. (*Thumbs at the kitchen.*)

MRS SHAW (*off*). Oh, don't worry. They know you of old.

SHAW (*calls*). Are you making us some tea, then, love?

MRS SHAW (*off*). I am. I won't be a minute.

SHAW. Heart of gold. Never stops working ... Was that your
car that Mrs Burnett told us about? We've just come up with
her. She saw it down the road.

ANDREW. They'll bury that woman in a glass coffin.

SHAW. Aye. If she couldn't look out she'd never step inside.

COLIN. Well, then, Steve. How's your writing going?

STEVEN. Oh, all right.

COLIN. Me mother said in her last letter you were going to pub-
lish a book.

STEVEN. I was. Sort of.

COLIN. Well, then. I'll look forward to seeing it.

SHAW. Aye. He's got all the brains, has Steven.

ANDREW. And all the kiddies too.

SHAW. Aye! (*He laughs*) Are you all right in there, love? (*Winks.*)

MRS SHAW (*off*). I'm all right. Don't you worry.

SHAW. They ought to run tea in pipes round here. Instead of
water.

COLIN. They'd make a fortune.

SHAW. Round here they would. (*Coughs*) Slakes your throat, you
know. Dust.

ANDREW. Sounds as though you've got half a ton of best nugget
down there, Dad.

SHAW. I have. Don't worry. I shouldn't be surprised.

STEVEN. My mother keeps telling him. He ought to come out.

SHAW. Come out. When I come out of that pit they can't tell the
difference between me and a lump of muck. Never get out of
that. Don't worry.

COLIN. I'll go see if my mother needs some help. (*Goes into
kitchen.*)

29

ANDREW (*gestures grandly after him*). Executive.

STEVEN. Nice bit of coat. (*Fingers it over a chair.*)

SHAW. You won't find one of them where I work, I can tell you.

ANDREW. I don't know. They tell me miners earn as much as dentists these days.

SHAW. What? At the bloody dogs they might. That's the only place they can.

ANDREW. I've even thought of going down myself.

SHAW. You've got a career you have. I spent half my life making sure none of you went down that pit.

ANDREW. I've always thought, you know, coal-mining was one of the few things I could really do. (*Looks at his hands*) One of the few things, in reality, for which I'm ideally equipped. And yet, the one thing in life from which I'm actually excluded.

SHAW. You're ideally equipped to be a professional man. Or owt you want. But that place: an animal could do what I do. And I can tell you, most of them are.

ANDREW. Aye. You're right. (*Snarls at* STEVEN, *then picks up one of the paperbacks*) Been studying your library.

STEVEN. One of the first things I ever remember was a picture in one of them. A cowboy with a hat out here and trousers flapping like wings, mounted on the back of a rearing horse. Somehow, it still sums it all up.

ANDREW. What?

STEVEN. Dunno ... Freedom. (*Pause.*)

SHAW. They're nowt. They pass the time.

ANDREW. I bet you can't remember a single one ... What happens ... (*Consults the book*) ... at Bloodstone Creek when Barry Hogan rides up and sees a light glinting from amongst the rocks?

SHAW. I couldn't tell you.

ANDREW. You're stunted. That's what you are.

SHAW. I am. It's a wonder I've grown one foot at all. (*They laugh*)

MRS SHAW (*returning*). Here we are ... Colin's bringing it in ...
(COLIN *follows her with the tray.*)

ANDREW. He'd make a lovely mother.

SHAW. You want to watch him. Or he'll shove it right over your head.

ANDREW. Couldn't knock a fly off a rice pudding.

COLIN. Don't be too sure.

ANDREW. He'd negotiate with it first.

MRS SHAW (*to* STEVEN). You're a quiet one, love. I hope you didn't let your Dad persuade you to have too much to drink.

STEVEN. No ...

SHAW. He doesn't say so much, but he doesn't miss owt do you, lad?

COLIN. How's your book going, then, Steve?
(COLIN *has put the tray on the table and* MRS SHAW *is pouring out the tea.*)

STEVEN. Oh, all right ... Well, not really. I've packed it in.

COLIN. Packed it in? Why, it's years ...

STEVEN. Aye.

SHAW. Why have you given it up, then, lad?

STEVEN. Not my cup of tea. (*Laughs*) Stick to what I've got, I suppose.

SHAW. Aye ... (SHAW *watches him.*)

MRS SHAW. He's better off looking after his wife and family, not writing books ...

COLIN. What was it all about, then, Steve?

STEVEN. Oh ... (*Shrugs.*)

ANDREW. Modern society. To put it into words.

STEVEN. I don't know. (*Shrugs.*)

ANDREW. Indicating, without being too aggressive, how we'd all succumbed to the passivity of modern life, industrial discipline, and moral turpitude.

MRS SHAW. Don't mock him.

ANDREW. I'm not mocking him. (*Spreads out his hands*) He let me read a bit of it once. What? Four years ago. He's been writing it nearly seven. I don't know why he's packed it in. I agree with every word.

SHAW. Agree with what?

ANDREW. I don't know ... his view of society. The modern world ...

SHAW. Nay, I can't make head nor tail of it ...

MRS SHAW. Here you are, love ... Come and get your tea.

MRS BURNETT (*popping in*). Are you in, love? Or are you out?

SHAW. We're out ... Don't worry. We've had her in here afore.

MRS SHAW. We're in, love. Don't take any notice.

MRS BURNETT. He never changes, does he? (To COLIN, *putting out her hand*) We hear all about you, now, you know.

COLIN. Not too much, I hope.

MRS BURNETT. No, no. Just the right things. What your father wants to tell us.

SHAW. Nay. Don't worry. I tell her nowt.

MRS BURNETT (*turning*). How are you, Andrew? I hear you've given up your job.

ANDREW. Aye. That's right. If you've aught going round here, just let me know.

MRS BURNETT. Get on with you. (*Laughs, digs him with her elbow*) That'll be the day, when he comes looking for a job round here.

ANDREW. It'll be sooner than you think. Don't worry. We're thinking of setting up in business.

MRS BURNETT. Business? What sort of business, then, is that?

ANDREW. Glass coffins.

MRS BURNETT. Glass coffins?

ANDREW. Or wooden ones. With little windows in. (*Shapes one.*)

MRS SHAW. Would you like a cup of tea, then, love?

MRS BURNETT. I wouldn't mind. I wouldn't say no ...

SHAW (*to himself*). Like asking a dog if it wants a pittle.

MRS BURNETT. I remember Colin. Mischief Night ...

ANDREW. Mischief Night? What mischief then has Colin ever got into?

MRS BURNETT. He's shoved some crackers through my back door a time or two. I can tell you that.

COLIN. I think I did. She's right. (*Laughs.*)

MRS BURNETT. And drain-pipes. Right along this street ... And Steven.

MRS SHAW. Steven?

STEVEN. Aye. I think I must.

ANDREW. It's coming out. Good God! I wouldn't believe it.

COLIN. Rafts on the canal. I remember that.

(*To* STEVEN.)

STEVEN. Aye ...

COLIN. We shoved our Steven in a time or two. It's a wonder he wasn't drowned.

STEVEN. Aye ...

SHAW. What about them kites, then, eh? Six foot. Fly for miles. You'd see them floating across the town when you went out shopping. Me. Reardon ... We used to give the lads half a crown to go climbing for them when they broke away ... It took two men to hold them. The string ... It could cut clean through your hand.

MRS BURNETT. Aye. I remember those days right enough ... And now look at you. Children of your own. (*To* MRS SHAW) It must be a proud day, love, for both of you ... Forty years.

MRS SHAW. Aye ...

SHAW. We'd have waited until we'd been married fifty, only I didn't think either of us would have lasted that long.

MRS SHAW. Oh, now ...

SHAW. At least, I didn't think I would ... We thought we'd better get it in while we had the chance.

MRS SHAW. Nay, I don't think it's as bad as that, love.

SHAW. Forty years. A round number ... I'm near retiring – God willing ... what with one thing and another ... Their mother's going to be ... well, I won't say, now, exactly ... but a *certain age* next week.

MRS SHAW. I'll be sixty. I don't mind them knowing.

SHAW. She was a young lass of twenty when I married her. And in my eyes, she's been the same age ever since.

MRS SHAW. Oh, now. Don't let's exaggerate too much.

SHAW. You're as old as you feel, and that's how I'll always see you, love. (*Kisses her cheek.*)

MRS SHAW. Nay, I don't know. He says some funny things ...

MRS BURNETT. Did you get your new hat, then?

MRS SHAW. I did.

SHAW. We'll have to go without food for a fortnight, I can tell you that.

MRS BURNETT. Oh, you'll look lovely, love.

SHAW. She'll look a picture. And for me she can dress up in rags.

MRS SHAW. I could as well. He wouldn't know the difference.

SHAW. Nay, we've gone without, I know. Getting these three into the world, setting them up in life.

MRS BURNETT. They're a credit to you, love. They are.

SHAW. Aye. Moments like this you begin to think it was all worth while. (*They laugh.*)

MRS SHAW. Oh, now ... Just look at the time.

SHAW. Aye. We shall have to be getting ready.

MRS BURNETT. 'The Excelsior Hotel.'

SHAW. That's the one.

MRS BURNETT (*to* COLIN). They only finished it last year. Twelve storeys high.

SHAW. It cost you a pound just to take your coat off. If you sneeze it costs you a fiver. And if you ask for a glass of water you've to tip ten bob just to pour it out. I tell you, I'm in the wrong bloody business. (*They laugh.*)

MRS BURNETT. Aye ... Well ... I'm only sorry your Jamey never lived to see it.

SHAW. Aye. Yes.

MRS BURNETT. He was a lovely lad. He was.

SHAW. We'd have been all right with four of them. We would.

MRS BURNETT. They wouldn't remember him.

SHAW. Aye. Well. You have your tribulations.

MRS BURNETT (*to* STEVEN). Missed him, you did, by about three months ... And Colin here ...

MRS SHAW. He'd be almost two. Andrew here was nearly five ...

MRS BURNETT (*to* ANDREW). Now, he could have been an artist. He could draw like a little angel. How old was he?

MRS SHAW. Seven when he died.

SHAW. He had a little book. His teacher sent it home. Drawings ... You wouldn't have known they hadn't been done by an artist. Shapes and colours ... There was one of three apples on a plate. You could almost pick them up ... Pneumonia ... They didn't have the protection against it, not in those days. Not like they have now ... I'd have cut off my right arm. I bloody would ... (*Sees* MRS SHAW'*s expression*) Aye ... Well ... (*Brightly*) Right, then ... (*Claps his hands*) Let's be ready. On with the dance.

MRS BURNETT. Aye. Well, I better be getting back ...

ANDREW. How are your lads, then, Mrs Burnett?

MRS BURNETT. Oh, well enough. Half a dozen kiddies. Not two minutes to come up and see their mother ... Still. That's how it is. (*To* MRS SHAW) That's where you're lucky, love. Your lads come home. Don't disown you. Don't forget you as you're getting old.

SHAW. Aye. We've been damn lucky.

MRS BURNETT (*to* MRS SHAW). If you drop your key off, love, I'll make sure your fire's in when you get back home.

MRS SHAW. Right, love ...

MRS BURNETT. Don't do anything I wouldn't do.

SHAW. That doesn't leave us with so bloody much.

MRS BURNETT (*to the others*). Tara, love. I'm off before he starts. (*Goes.*)

COLIN. One of the best. She is.

ANDREW. One of the best what?

COLIN. Forget it ...

ANDREW. You should have heard him in the car. Talk about the Two Nations. The dignity of the manual labourer.

SHAW. Labourer?

COLIN. I should forget it.

ANDREW. Never ask an expatriate working-class man about his views on his former class. Do you know, when he left school and went to university, Colin was a card-carrying member of the C.P.

MRS SHAW (*clearing cups*). C.P.? What's that?

STEVEN. A communist.

MRS SHAW. A communist!

ANDREW. To my mother, communist is synonymous with sex deviate, pervert, luster after young girls, defiler of young men.

MRS SHAW. I never said that ... I never knew you were a communist, Colin.

ANDREW. Neither did he. It only lasted a year. It gives him an aura of respectability now when he's negotiating with 'the men'.

COLIN. You'd go down well, I can tell you.

ANDREW. Down well what? I've gone down. You can't get much lower than where I am, mate.

SHAW. We're here to celebrate, not to have arguments. (*To* MRS SHAW) I remember when they were all at home. Arguments! It was like a debating palace. Your head got dizzy following each one.

MRS SHAW. Well, I'll get up and get changed. I suppose all you are ready?

COLIN. Yes ... Here, I'll take that. (*Indicating tray.*)

MRS SHAW. No, no. I've got it, love ... Harry? (*Goes.*)

SHAW. Aye. I better put on my suit. They might throw me out if I go as I am. 'The Excelsior.' Do you know, the man on the door, dressed up like an admiral – that much braid and epaulets on that he knocks your eye out whenever he turns round – he used to work for me. Swore like a trooper and never washed his face from one Sunday to the next. There he is now, dressed up for a coronation, with a spot of scent behind his ears. 'Why!' I said to him when I last went past, 'You're like a bloody woman, Alf. Get off home and get some clothes on.' Do you know what he said? 'If you don't move on, my man, I'll have you physically removed.' 'Physically removed'?

ANDREW. Did you sock him one?

SHAW. Sock him? I wouldn't have muckied my hands. (*They laugh.*) Ay, look, you know. About Jamey ... I shouldn't talk about him too much. I know you didn't bring it up, but your mother, you know ... as you get older you start thinking about these things.

COLIN. What about them?

SHAW. Nay, look ... I've said enough. (*Listens. Then, loudly*) Right, then, lads. I'll go get polished up.

ANDREW. Leave a bit of muck on, Dad. We won't know you without.

SHAW. Aye. Some hopes of that. (*Gestures up*) I'll be given a thorough inspection ...

ANDREW. Hygiene ...

SHAW. Hygiene. You're right. (*Laughs*) Right, then. I'll get up ... Think on ... (*Goes.*)

ANDREW (*cheerful*). Well, then: this time tomorrow we'll all be back home.

COLIN. I should just lay off, you know. Just once. Give it a rest.

ANDREW. Are you going to negotiate with me or something, Colin?

COLIN. We're here to give them a good time. Something they'll remember. God alone knows they deserve it.

ANDREW. Aye. He's right. How about you, Steve? What're you so quiet about? (STEVEN *shrugs*) Silent Steven. (*To* COLIN) They called him that at school.

COLIN. I've just thought. I'll have all that way to walk back to get the car.

STEVEN. Ring for a taxi.

COLIN. It's the same distance to the phone box, the other way.

ANDREW. You forget, don't you, what a primitive place this really is. Do you know, the other morning, we ran out of toothpaste at home, and there was all hell let loose with Pete – he's courting his head-girl at school – and I suddenly remembered: we never had toothpaste at home. Do you remember? We all used to clean our teeth with salt. (*Laughs*) Three little piles on the draining board every morning, when we came down.

STEVEN. We never had any cakes either. Do you remember that? There was a jam tart, or one piece of a sponge roll, for tea on Sunday.

COLIN. And old Steve there used to stand at table because we only had four chairs.

ANDREW. I remember. Would you believe it. (*They look round at the room*) Do you remember when old Shuffler came to see my Dad about my going to university?

STEVEN. Shuffler?

COLIN. He'd left by the time you'd got there.

ANDREW. Sixth form. Careers. Came here one night to talk to my Dad about 'the pros and cons' of going to university. Sat in a chair: we had it there. Put his hands out like this and … ping! Bloody springs shot out.

COLIN. Nearly dislocated his elbow! (*They laugh.*)

ANDREW (*laughing*). And my Dad ... my Dad said to him ... 'Would you mind not putting your hands on the arms, Mr Rushton? ... The springs are coming out!' (*They laugh.*)

COLIN. Bare floors. We had a piece of lino which my mother moved round each week, trying to fit the chairs over the holes and spaces.

STEVEN. Newspaper on the table for dinner ...

ANDREW. Breakfast, supper and tea.

STEVEN. 'Don't read when you're eating.' (*They laugh.*)

COLIN. Do you remember my mother cutting up newspapers into lengths and trying to roll them together like a proper toilet roll? (*They laugh.*)

ANDREW. Obsessive man.

COLIN. After he came here Shuffler never talked to us again. Whenever we met in the school corridor he used to gaze at some point exactly six inches above your head. Talk about the pain of poverty. I still dream about that look. I do ... I often wake up trying to convince him that we're not as poor as that any longer. (*Pause.*)

ANDREW. That comes of going to a good school.

COLIN. Full of drapers' sons, minor bureaucrats, and the children of the professional classes.

ANDREW. My dear old Col: your children are the children of the professional classes.

COLIN. I have no children.

ANDREW. Good God. You haven't. I'd forgot.

STEVEN. Why have you never married, Colin?

COLIN. Don't know. Haven't had the time.

ANDREW. You're not ... er ... ? (*Quivers his hand.*)

COLIN. Don't think so.

ANDREW. I mean, if you are, for my mother's sake, I'd keep it under your hat.

COLIN. Oh, sure.

ANDREW (*to* STEVEN). It's one thing my mother cannot stand. 'I don't mind a man being as promiscuous as he likes' – within reason, of course, and with the sole exception of my dad – 'but the thought of one man going with another ...'

COLIN. I don't think we've quite come to that ... In any case, as far as marriage is concerned, I probably might have to.

ANDREW. You don't mean ... there's not some unfortunate lassie carrying an embryonic Colin in her tum ...

COLIN. No. It's just less embarrassing to *be* married than not to be.

ANDREW. I see. Well. As long as it's only that.

COLIN. Yes.

ANDREW. You know the real reason he's never married.

COLIN. No. I don't think he does.

ANDREW. Well. Never mind ... Forget it ...

STEVEN. In any case ...

ANDREW. Yes?

STEVEN. With all that money lying around, Colin, you ought to make some woman happy.

COLIN. Aye! (*Laughs.*)

(ANDREW *watches* STEVEN *a moment. Then:*)

ANDREW. What's gone wrong, then, Steve?

STEVEN. I don't know what you mean there, Andy. (*Moves about the room, casual.*)

ANDREW. I mean ... I don't know what I mean.

COLIN (*to* STEVEN). He's not sure what he means.

ANDREW. For one thing ... in your youth ... you were so contemptuous of the proven way.

COLIN. The proven way ...

ANDREW. Admittedly you were – for ever – silent. But even when at school – the school we have, only a moment before described, fit only for the sons of Christ – and then only after the most rigorous scrutiny – your arrogance, your disdain ... your *contempt* – were there for everyone to see ... I know.

I know. Actually I respected you – very much – because of that. Misplaced it may have been – contempt ... God knows: the educated sons of that school, Steve, deserved all the pity they could get. But you – just look at you. Where oh where has all that venom gone to? Where, for Christ's sake, Steve, is the spirit of revenge? (STEVEN *shrugs*.)

COLIN. Four hours of that I've had inside that car ... You should have heard him ... If you ever have a car don't ever let him in it. Two miles with him in the passenger seat and you'll drive it into the nearest wall.

ANDREW. Though in his case, of course, he's more appreciative of the cost.

COLIN. You know, your one grievous disability, Andy – if you don't mind me mentioning this – is not only have you never grown up, but you've never even put in the first preliminary effort.

ANDREW (*to* STEVEN). 'Management' talk. His 'men's' talk is both more subtly obscene and more overtly gratuitous.

COLIN. I must say, it's come to a sorry bloody pitch. (*To* STEVEN) I could have got him a job years ago if he'd wanted. I could have even got him on the board; what with his gifts, his tongue, his golden sense of opportunity. He might even have done him a bit of good.

ANDREW. You are listening to a man whose life – believe it or not – is measured out in motor cars.

COLIN. In blood! In men! In progress!

ANDREW. Do you know what he told me on the way up here? Cigar in mouth. Gloved hands firmly on the wheel. 'The well-being of this nation is largely – if not wholly – dependent on maintaining a satisfactory level of exports from the motor industry.' The *nation*! ... If my bloody nation is largely dependent on that I'd rather crawl around on all fours with a pig-skin on my back and a bow and arrow in my bloody hand. I would.

COLIN. You probably might have to. (*Laughs pleasantly.*) Sooner than he thinks.

ANDREW. May God speed that day. (*Looks up.*) May God speed it.

COLIN. And that mind you after witnessing my poor old father's life. Crawling around – in pitch black, on his belly, his life hanging on the fall of a piece of rock – for fifty bloody years!

ANDREW. My father – *old friend* – has more dignity in his little finger than all you and your automated bloody factories could conjure up in a thousand years.

COLIN. Yes?

ANDREW. You know, I weep for you. To think you once lived here, under this roof. My brother. And you end up ... Just look at you ... Like this.

COLIN (*goes to the stairs*). Are you ready, then, up there?

SHAW (*off*). Nay, damn it all. We're trying to fasten your mother's dress.

MRS SHAW (*off*). Don't worry, love. We won't be long.

(COLIN *goes to the kitchen: starts to wash as:*)

ANDREW. I'm not trying to disparage, Steve ... your work. Your ideas ... It's simply: I do not understand.

STEVEN. No.

ANDREW. What's happened to that re-vitalizing spirit? To the iconoclast, to use my mother's word.

STEVEN. I don't know.

ANDREW. Steve!

STEVEN. Look. There's no hard and fast rule. The world's as real as anything else: you don't ... compromise yourself by taking a part in it.

ANDREW. No? ... Not even with *this* world, Steve? (*Gestures through at* COLIN.)

STEVEN. No. It's not essential.

ANDREW. And that's why you look as sick as you do, because that's something you believe?

STEVEN. I look as sick as I do – if I do look sick – because I'm not a moralist like you. In the end, attitudes like you've described are easily adopted. All you have to do is throw over what's already there. You're like an evangelist. You both are. You forget there's another kind of temperament.

ANDREW. Well ...

STEVEN. I don't know what the word for it is. (*Turns away.*)

ANDREW. Have you ever thought of taking up welfare work?

STEVEN. What?

ANDREW. The *all-surveying eye* – inherited – I haven't a shadow of a doubt – from my mother, but used, also I have no doubt, with greater circumspection – isn't this something you could put to better use than ... advising on – what is it? – suitable post-graduate, post-everything pursuits?

STEVEN. I don't know.

ANDREW. But for the fact that I almost witnessed the event, I would find it difficult to believe that you came, as it were, of man and woman, Steve. Dearly as I would like, myself, to be an intellectual ...

STEVEN (*to* COLIN). Intellectual ... (*Laughs*)

ANDREW (*through to* COLIN). Whenever one such passes me in the street, whenever I meet a man who describes himself as a humanist, a rationalist, a man of reason, something in my soul, something deep inside me, calls out – in pain, in protest. 'This man,' it tells me, 'is *obscene*.'

COLIN (*coming in, drying face*). It seems there's an awful lot of obscenity in your life, Andy.

ANDREW (*to* STEVEN). When you see a cancer it's no commendation of your powers of loving to fall on your knees and give it a damn great kiss.

COLIN (*to* STEVEN). He'll kill us all off. He will. He really will.

ANDREW. We already are.

COLIN. What?

ANDREW. Dead. Zombies. Killed by good intentions, administered by the ones above. (*Gestures up.*) Corpses.

COLIN (*lightly*). Good God ... What's he on about, then, Steve?

STEVEN. I don't know ... It's not worth arguing about. I remember, when he first started grammar school ...

ANDREW. Minor public. It said that in the brochure ... (*to* COLIN) My dad underlined it with black, colliery crayon.

STEVEN. He came home and devastated all of us – me certainly, without a shadow of a doubt – with all the reasons why it was no longer tenable – a belief in God. As if belief itself were a kind of property, like a limb, which you could put on or take off at will ... Believe me: remove any part and all the rest goes with it. I don't even understand ... You've lived here half your life – Reardon – Mrs Burnett – even Shuffler ... What sort of vengeance do you have in mind?

ANDREW. Are you *listening* to what I said? (STEVEN *nods.*) ... God knows, you were always the most serious of the three – and God knows, there were sufficient reasons for it ...

COLIN (*pulling on coat, etc.*). What *is* all this? What reasons? What God knows? ... I must say, for somebody who doesn't believe in God he invokes Him an awful bloody lot ... you know ... Formative traits have always been an obsession with our Andrew: as if he were a function of them and nothing else ...

ANDREW. All right ... (*turns away.*)

COLIN. Good God. (*Takes his tie from his pocket and starts to put it on.*) Amazing.

ANDREW. When poor old Jamey died ...

COLIN. I knew it!

ANDREW. When poor old Jamey died ...

COLIN (*to* STEVEN). Do we have to go through all this again?

STEVEN. Andrew has a new theory about his origins.

ANDREW. Not new. And not theoretical, either.

STEVEN. He's discovered ... I told him. A little time ago now ...

that Jamey was born only three months after my mother got married.

COLIN (*putting on tie*). Good Lord. (*Feels walls*) No. No. Upright ... Standing.

ANDREW. Can you imagine, for one moment, what went on during those six months' negotiations? Prior to the event.

COLIN. ... Let me see.

ANDREW. This is something you should be particularly good at ... I mean: first in human hygiene ...

COLIN. Why does he go *on* about that?

ANDREW. English language, domestic science: didn't leave school until she was sixteen ... religious ... raised up by a petty farmer to higher things ... ends up being laid – in a farm field – by a bloody collier ... hygiene ... never forgiven him, she hasn't ... Dig coal he will till kingdom come. Never dig enough ... Retribution.

COLIN. Do you know what I'd say to you?

ANDREW. What?

COLIN. Mind your own bleeding business.

ANDREW. Oh ... All right. (*Turns away.* COLIN *goes off.*) Poor old Jamey.

COLIN. (*off*). Poor old Jamey ...

ANDREW. Poor old Dad.

COLIN. Poor old Dad. (*Reappearing with waistcoat: and jacket – which he puts on a chair.*)

ANDREW. Well, that's it exactly.

COLIN. What?

ANDREW. Guilt. Subsequent moral rectitude. They fashioned Jamey – as a consequence – in the image of Jesus Christ.

COLIN. I can think of worse examples. (*Goes to mirror to check tie.*)

ANDREW. Yes?

COLIN. Well – I wouldn't wish to get too personal. (*Laughs.*)

ANDREW. No. No. On the other hand?

COLIN. On the other hand …

ANDREW. Christ didn't take too kindly to Jamey. His was not, after all, a messianic role.

COLIN (*to* STEVEN). 'When Mary said, "We have a son," her husband said, "Tell me another one." '

STEVEN. Andrew thinks Jamey died because he could never atone …

COLIN. Atone? For what?

STEVEN. I don't know … Whatever my mother felt …

COLIN. He died of pneumonia, according to the certificate. I remember seeing it myself, years ago. (*Looks round for his jacket.*)

ANDREW. He died from a bout of galloping perfection.

COLIN. Did he?

ANDREW. Do you remember Jamey?

COLIN. Not really … I was only two or three at the time …
(*To* STEVEN. *Picks up his jacket and puts it on.*)

ANDREW. I was nearly five. I remember him very well. Sitting there … drawing … Or upstairs. Crying. They never beat us, you know. But him … he was black and blue … And like Steven there – but for his little bloody pictures – *silent as the tomb.* (*To* STEVEN) … Come on.

COLIN. Come on? Come on what? Honestly, the way he dramatizes the slightest inflection. Black and blue. I don't remember that. And I remember my Dad landing *me* one once or twice, I do … (*To* STEVEN) And you.
(STEVEN *doesn't answer.*)
Well?
(STEVEN *shrugs.*)

ANDREW. Come on. Fair's fair. If Colin's going to whitewash everything, why not give him every chance?

STEVEN. It's nothing …

ANDREW. Nothing … ?

STEVEN (*shrugs*). It's nothing.

ANDREW (*to* COLIN). Years ago ...

STEVEN. Years ago ...

ANDREW. My dad ...

STEVEN. My father ... it's really nothing ... (*Sees* ANDREW's *look*) ... He told me – shortly after Jamey died – my mother tried ...

COLIN. What?

ANDREW. To kill herself.

(STEVEN *turns away.*)

ANDREW. Oh, no. Fair's fair. Look ... She was already six months gone with Steve ... sitting here ... on the floor ... hugging a knife ... when the old man staggers in through that very door ...

COLIN. Not drunk ... ?

ANDREW. From work ... You see, this doesn't interest him at all.

COLIN. Do you think, in all honesty, that it should? All right ... she tried to kill herself.

ANDREW. You already knew.

COLIN. Yes. That's right. I already knew ... She told me ... Years ago. I can't remember.

ANDREW. Well, then. That's that.

COLIN. All right. She tried to kill herself.

ANDREW. And Steve.

COLIN. And Steve ... He wasn't even born.

ANDREW. No. No. He wasn't ... Waiting there, that's all ... *To be delivered* ... Just look at him ... Still waiting ... Solemn ... Silent.

COLIN. All right. All right ... I mean ... poor bloody soul ... is it something I should bear with me, every second, every day? ... I mean ... are we supposed to be endlessly, perpetually measured by our bloody imperfections, by our more unfortunate bloody actions? ... Just what precisely are you after, Andy? Do you want somebody to hold your hand throughout your entire bloody life?

ANDREW. Ask Steve.

COLIN. What about 'ask Steve'? He's more bloody commonsense. For Christ's sake. You really take the can.

ANDREW. Ask Steve ... (*To* STEVEN) Tell him ... Go on ... I mean, giving up his book isn't really what you'd think ... a sign of his growing up ... maturity. He actually has been having nightmares ... In true, I might add, evangelical style.

COLIN. Nightmares? What about?

ANDREW. Jamey ... He sees him – crying out ... trying to appease the immaculate conception. Trying to tell them it *wasn't his fault* ... Jamey in the wilderness, Jamey on a mountain top, Jamey at the window ... saying ... 'Even if you were first in human hygiene, and intended marrying someone smarter than my dad, it wasn't my fault. Please God, forgive me ... Please ... God forgive me, Ma! It's not my fault.'

(COLIN *looks at* STEVEN *who shakes his head.*)

COLIN. What's he on about?

ANDREW. He wrote me a letter recently, Steven. I say recently. Some months ago – and I apologize for taking over ... appropriating, his pre-natal, post-natal, pre-genetive feelings of contempt – I'm sorry, in fact if I appear to sit in judgment on his suffering, on his perpetual psychic silences ... but that sickness, I should add, is a disease of mine. His affliction, I can assure him, is not endemic to his solemn, silent nature, atrophied while inside my mother's remorseful tum ... Jamey's cry, I can assure him, comes from the family! ... not just from his own, sleeping, nocturnal soul ...

COLIN. What's he ...?

ANDREW. Colin's trouble is that he can't put an engine inside his consternation and drive it off ... *Good old Col!* Something has actually struck home at last.

COLIN. Look ... I've had enough. Just pack it in. For Christ's sake ... Steve.

STEVEN. It's nothing. I wrote Andy a letter a few months back. A year ... Asking what he thought. Revenge, I'm afraid, is his only answer. And I understand his motives well enough ...

COLIN. Revenge? On what?

STEVEN. On them.

COLIN. On them ... For what?

STEVEN. I don't know ... Everything.

COLIN. I see ... Nothing less than that.

ANDREW. Projecting him into a world they didn't understand. Educating him for a society which existed wholly in their imaginations ... philistine, parasitic, opportunistic ... bred in ignorance, fed in ignorance ... dead – in ignorance.

STEVEN. Only, of course, his commonsense – perhaps even his compassion – forbids him to say anything of the sort ... The most tedious thing about his social attitudes, his moral insights, is the perversity of their motives – that's something I've always felt before about these screaming revolutionaries ... but now ... I see more clearly what they're intended to appease.

ANDREW (to STEVEN). We'll build a bloody statue to you yet. I'm warning you. We shall ... He thinks by some superb gesture of self-exorcism, powered and engendered by God knows what, he'll rid himself of all this. His dreams and nightmares ...

STEVEN (quietly). No ...

ANDREW. Transcend it. Become ... manifest.

STEVEN. No ...

ANDREW. I think, you know, some suitable post should be found for Steven. (To COLIN) He'll do you out of a job, if you're not careful. Don't let him near your factory. He'll have everybody, unless you're very careful, consoling one another.

STEVEN. Yes. Well ...

ANDREW. You're like a man with one foot on either side of an ever-widening chasm. The kind of detachment – or even the kind of *involvement* – you're telling me about: very soon, as your looks suggest ... is going to rip you wide apart. You can't be *for* this crummy world and at the same time be for your own psychic ... spiritual ... *moral* autonomy, any longer. It is now the season of the locusts, and if you have anything to save then save it. Grab it in both hands and run.

STEVEN. Yes ... well.

ANDREW. Well? Well, what?

STEVEN. Let's hope there aren't too many of you.

ANDREW. Too many?

STEVEN. Someone has to stay behind.

ANDREW. Behind? You're not behind. You're nowhere You're *overrun*.

SHAW (*off*). Well then ... Well, then ... Here I come ...

COLIN (*to* ANDREW). Forget it. (*Calling*) Do you want a hand, or can you manage?

SHAW (*off*). I don't damn well know ... ooh! (*Groans.*)

COLIN (*to* ANDREW). Look. Just lay off ...

(ANDREW *begins to whistle a tune, wandering round the room, his hands in his pockets.*

SHAW *comes in, in his best suit, dark blue, and a little old-fashioned in cut. He carries his shoes in his hand.*)

SHAW. By go. These braces. They're like a straitjacket on your back ... Your mother won't be a minute. I had to hang around to give her a hand. Can't reach any of her buttons these days, you know. Oooh! (*Sits down to put on his shoes*) Just look at that. (*Holds up a shoe*) She's had me polishing that since a week last Sunday. If you shone a light on it it'd burn your eyes.

(*They laugh, looking at one another.*)

COLIN. Look ... I better fetch the car.

SHAW. Aye. I was thinking of that ... Can you wait till she

comes down? She wants to make 'an entry'. She'll be another half an hour after that, doing her gloves up, getting her hair right. So you'll be all right.

COLIN. Aye. Well. There's no great hurry. We'll have a drive around.

SHAW. She'd like that. She's been on at me to get a car. At my age. I can't bloody see a lamp-post till it hits me in the face ... She's had a hard life. She's worked very hard. Kept this like a palace ... One woman in a house of men. She'd have given aught, you know, to have had a daughter. You know, somebody to talk to ... Ay up. Here She's coming.

(*He gets up to take up a casual pose by the fireplace, winking at the others.*)

MRS SHAW (*off*). Are you ready?

SHAW. Aye. We're ready, love. We've been waiting here for hours.

MRS SHAW (*off*). Ups! Won't be a minute.

SHAW (*to the others*). Last-minute hitch.

(*They're standing now in their respective places round the room, facing the door.*)

MRS SHAW (*off*). Are you ready, then?

COLIN. We're ready.

SHAW. Here she comes ...

(*Pause. Then* MRS SHAW *appears at the door. She wears a dignified blue costume, her coat folded neatly over her arm. In one hand is a pair of white gloves and a handbag. On her head is a matching blue hat, not ostentatious.*)

COLIN. Wow!

ANDREW. Lovely.

SHAW. Beautiful.

MRS SHAW. Do you like it?

STEVEN. It's very nice. I couldn't have done better myself. (*He embraces her.*)

COLIN. Super ... smashing. (COLIN *embraces her.*)

SHAW. Here ... better give her a kiss an' all. (*Kisses her modestly on the cheek.*)

ANDREW. Well, then. Are we ready?

COLIN. I'll go fetch the car.

MRS SHAW. Nay, well, look ... Let's all walk down. It's only half a mile.

COLIN. Well ...

ANDREW. Do you feel up to it?

(SHAW *and* COLIN *laugh.*)

MRS SHAW. We've walked down that road together often enough in the past. Once more won't do us any hurt.

(COLIN *holds the coat and she puts it on.*)

(*To* SHAW) Can you lock the door?

SHAW. Aye. Aye ... I'll just get my coat. (*Goes.*)

COLIN. Have we to go in front, or do we follow on behind? (*Pulling on his own coat.*)

MRS SHAW. Well, I don't know.

COLIN. Here you are, then. (*Offers her his arm*) We'll go in front. Show the flag.

MRS SHAW. Have you all got your coats?

STEVEN (*pulling his on*). That's an old familiar question.

COLIN. Cleaned your shoes? Washed your faces? Ties straight? Got your handkerchief? Right, then: have you all got your coats?

(*They laugh.*)

SHAW (*returning, his coat on*). All locked up. Ready.

COLIN (*leading* MRS SHAW *the other way*). Nay, out of the front door today, Mother. Dad – bring up the rear.

(COLIN *goes with* MRS SHAW *on his arm.*)

SHAW. Bring up the rear, he says. Who's boss here, I'm thinking.

ANDREW. You and me, old lad. (*Puts his arm round* SHAW'*s shoulder*) Come on, Steve ... We're not leaving you at home.

(ANDREW *and* SHAW *go.* STEVEN *remains a moment, buttoning his coat.*

He pauses: looks round.)

MRS SHAW (*off*). Steven?

(*He looks round the room once more.*
Then, slowly, he moves to the door and goes, closing it behind
him.)

FADE

ACT TWO

Scene 1

Late evening.

MRS BURNETT *comes in. She puts on the light, draws the curtains, looks in the kitchen, puts coal on the fire.*

Unseen by her, REARDON *puts his head round the door: an elderly man dressed in a neat suit, dark, a handkerchief in the top pocket, with gloves and a walking cane: an Irish accent, dandyish but by no means effete. He watches* MRS BURNETT *a moment. Then:*

REARDON. *Aha!*

MRS BURNETT. Ooh! (*Jumps, startled.*)

REARDON. Thought I saw a light. Burglars!

MRS BURNETT. Burglars. They'll be catching you one of these nights.

REARDON. Reardon? The one-man vigilante? ... (*Hastily looks round*) They haven't left a drop, have they, by any chance?

MRS BURNETT. They have not. And the key's in my possession for safe keeping. Not for letting strangers in and out.

REARDON (*with dignity*). Harry Shaw and I have been the closest friends for over thirty-five years.

MRS BURNETT. I know. And never closer than when he's standing at a bar.

REARDON. One man, one round. That has always been my motto. And what little secrets have you been prying out? (REARDON *is moving round the room inspecting.*)

MRS BURNETT. None. Not any. I have more respect for people's privacy than that. (*Shifts chairs, etc., as she talks*) I've been building up the fire. They'll be back soon, unless they're going to make a morning of it as well as half a night ... Now ... (*Gestures at him to stop prying.*)

REARDON. It's all right. It's all right. Didn't I meet them on the way down the street this evening? 'Good day,' says I, 'but that's a sight for sore eyes. Three famous sons taking out their mother and dad.'

Are you sure ... ? (*Gestures at the sideboard.*)

MRS BURNETT. If there was I wouldn't touch it. In all the years they've left me with the key I've never once touched anything in here, and I never shall.

REARDON. Harry Shaw and I have never allowed the perversity of private property to come between us. 'What is mine is yours, and what is yours is mine,' has always been our motto.

MRS BURNETT. Well, the same doesn't go for Mrs Shaw, and she's the one you have to make account to.

REARDON. That's true. There goes a woman before whom I shall always remove my hat.

MRS BURNETT. I should think so, too.

REARDON. Behind every great man, now, you find a promising woman.

MRS BURNETT. You do. Don't you forget it.

REARDON. Am I likely? The one deficiency in an otherwise phenomenal life. Your respect for the privileged classes does you credit, Mrs Burnett.

MRS BURNETT. Privileged?

REARDON. When the aspirations of the working classes are to join the lower middle, what do the Shaws do, but jump over a couple and land right up there, at the very top.

MRS BURNETT. The top?

REARDON. I wouldn't pretend, now, that they'd be aristocrats, within the one generation. But it wouldn't surprise me if one day, in the not too distant future, a Shaw is found sitting in the House of Lords, breathing down enlightenment on every side, a mind nurtured ... formed, inspired, within these four walls. So is a beacon lit, Mrs Burnett. And so are the great allowed to shed their light ... One of gin, one of sherry, one of soda water, and unless I am very much mistaken, a damn great one of Scotch. (*Has opened the sideboard cupboard door.*)

MRS BURNETT. I don't care whether there's a crate-ful. You're not touching a single drop. (*She steps in and shuts the cupboard door.*) I would have thought Mrs Reardon would have wanted you home in bed hours ago.

REARDON. Mrs Reardon, alas, Mrs Burnett, has not wanted me home in bed, or anywhere else for that matter, for more years than you and I could count together.

MRS BURNETT. Well, I'm sure …

REARDON. If my father had given me the opportunities that Mr Shaw has given to his sons, do you know where I would be now?

MRS BURNETT. I've no idea. It'd have a bar in it, I know that for sure.

REARDON. You're right. I would accumulate what little wealth my golden opportunities had provided and, splitting everything in half, I would retire …

MRS BURNETT. Retire?

REARDON. To the west coast of my native land, the wildness of which is past description. And from where, so many years ago I've lost count, my old father, God rest his soul, first brought me, a mewling infant in my mother's impoverished arms.

MRS BURNETT. And half would be for what?

REARDON. Half would be for building a modest little cottage, hewn from the rock from which my forebears sprang, the homeland of my fathers – stretching back into the very mists of time, before Christ, before the great dynasties of Egypt and Crete and Persia … those mist-shrouded, northern shores … where the sun rises like a holy fire …

MRS BURNETT. Well …

(REARDON *stands for a moment, gazing out, abstracted, one arm raised.*)

And the other half for what?

REARDON. The other half … ?

The other half, my dear. With that I shall build a deep, concrete, lead-lined, bomb-proof, a-tomic shelter.

MRS BURNETT. A shelter.

REARDON. Unlike Mr Shaw, I am past retiring age. Certain irregularities in the local office of the National Coal Board have allowed me to spend rather longer than legally I am entitled to in the colliery office, checking pay, attempting, in my own small way, to settle amicably the various disputes – soothing the manager's sorrow, the deputy's rage, appeasing whenever I could the miner's consternation … I have seen two world wars and several minor ones, and not a little of my life's energies have been expended in avoiding each and every one: I have lived through the most calamitous half-century since time began and my instinct for war, for rivalry and destruction, is unparalleled, I would imagine, by almost any-one. I have a vision, Mrs Burnett, a presentiment … of a holocaust so gigantic, so monumental in its proportions, that beside it all our little dreams and hopes, our sorrows, and our little aims and fears … must count as nothing. Whether these are the sort of visions endemic to a man very close to retiring age – and to a pension it can only humiliate him to receive – or whether they are a definitive view of reality as we and our children shall eventually come to know it – I cannot say. All I can see before me, I must confess, are flames – flames, pillage, burning, terror.

MRS BURNETT. You've been drinking. That's what you've seen: the bottom of too many glasses.

REARDON. When I retire to my bomb-proof shelter, Mrs Burnett, I will – if you'll grant me the privilege – take you with me. While the flames roar around our pathetic heads I shall take comfort from your good-natured incomprehen-sion and – who knows? – recognize in it maybe some hope and reassurance for the future. Only those who cannot – through their own intrinsic stupidity – appreciate that something calamitous is happening: only amongst those will I feel really safe.

MRS BURNETT. There they are. You see. (*Lifts curtain to look out*) I don't know what they're going to think to find somebody else in here ...

REARDON. I shall retire, Mrs Burnett. And who knows? A few moments later I might quite easily pop in my head as if I were, in a manner of speaking, passing by, on my way home, to my dear wife ... In all my life I have never been an embarrassment to anyone ... No. No ... and, if I can only manage it now, I never shall.

(*He goes off with a little bow, through the kitchen.*
Noises of Shaws off: MRS BURNETT *makes a last quick inspection.*
The door from the front opens. ANDREW *comes in.*)

ANDREW (*calling back*). No, no. It's Mrs Burnett. All safe. Come in ... (*To* MRS BURNETT) They thought they were being raided.

SHAW (*entering*). What did I tell you? ... By, that's lovely and warm.

MRS BURNETT. I thought it might be going out ...

SHAW. Aye ... aye.

MRS BURNETT. Have you had a nice time?

SHAW. Grand! Grand! Lovely ... Couldn't have been better.

(MRS SHAW *comes in on* STEVEN's *arm.*)

We have to hold her up. Got us nearly arrested.

MRS SHAW. Hold me up! I'm quite all right ... (*To* MRS BURNETT) It was very good of you, love. I appreciate it. That's a lovely fire.

MRS BURNETT. I've put the key on the sideboard.

SHAW. Nay, don't rush off yet. We're having a celebration, you know. Still got a drop put by.

MRS BURNETT. Well ...

SHAW (*to* MRS BURNETT). Best night of my life! 'Excelsior'?

Seen nothing like it. We had that many waiters running round
the table you couldn't see the food ... (*Belches.*)

MRS SHAW. Oh, now ...

SHAW. That's right, love. You sit down.

(MRS SHAW *is helped to a chair.*)

MRS SHAW. Oh ... (*To* MRS BURNETT) It's been lovely.

MRS BURNETT. Ey, I'm glad ...

MRS SHAW. The view ... All the walls are made of glass. On the
top floor, the restaurant. You can see right over the town.

SHAW. From the muck-heap at one end to the muck-heap at the
other.

MRS SHAW. It wasn't like that at all ... You can see the moors
from up there. Miles. Sweeping away. And rocks ... When
the sun set you could see the light – glinting on a stream ...
well, it must have been miles away.

STEVEN. Yes. That's right.

MRS SHAW. Beautiful. You'd have liked it ... When it got dark
all the lights came on. You could see right up the valley ...
Lines of lights. Little clusters ... And a train. Just like a snake
... winding in and out ... I don't know. We've lived here all
our lives and I've never seen it like that.

SHAW. We've skint our Colin. (*To* ANDREW) Isn't that right?

ANDREW. Aye! (*Laughs.*)

SHAW. He won't come up here again in a hurry, I can tell you.
Champagne? He's even got a bottle in the car. (*Takes*
MRS BURNETT'*s arm*) We tipped the doorman. Should have
seen his face. Remember Alf Dyson? He worked with me.
Face as black as a Christmas pudding. Never washed. 'Here
you are, my man,' I said, and doffed him a five pound note.
Our Colin's. You should have seen him. Nearly dropped his
medals in the road.

(*They laugh.*)

I bet there isn't a bottle left in that place. What's he up to?

(ANDREW *has been looking in the cupboards.*)

ANDREW. Trying to find it.

SHAW. Here. In here, old lad. A bit of space left for a drop more.

MRS SHAW. Not for me, thanks.

SHAW. Mrs Burnett. You'll have the first. We'll have another toast.

MRS BURNETT. Oh, well …

(REARDON *puts his head in from the door leading to the front.*)

REARDON. Did I hear … 'Toast'?

SHAW. Why! … Look what's here! Look what's here!

(REARDON *comes in, followed by* COLIN.)

COLIN. Found him skulking about outside …

REARDON. Just passing by. Saw a light. Thought: by jove, burglars! Apprehend …

SHAW. Nothing of the kind. (*To the others*) He can smell a drop of Scotch a mile off. We once went walking on the moors … this is just after I was married …

ANDREW. Already running off …

SHAW. Nay. Nay. I was always going for walks …

REARDON. He was.

SHAW. Got lost … Should have seen us. Moorland stretching round on every side.

REARDON. It was. Those were the great days of our life.

SHAW (*indicating* REARDON). 'Reardon. Which way is it to the nearest pub?'

(*They laugh.*)

He turns this way … (*Turns*) Then that. (*Turns*) Then he says, 'Harry. This is the road we want.'

(*They laugh.*)

REARDON. I did.

SHAW. And it was. Over the next rise and there we were.

REARDON. 'The Flying Horse.'

SHAW. 'The Flying Horse'! You're right!

REARDON. Never forget a name like that.

SHAW. No. No. Me neither. Not them sort, any road.

(*They've been pouring out the drinks and passing them round*)
Should have seen our Andrew.

REARDON. What's that?

MRS SHAW. Oh, better not ...

SHAW. Half way through the meal – restaurant full of people.

REARDON. Captains of industry, Harry.

SHAW. They were. They were. You're right. Mill-owners. Engineering managers. Leaders of our imports ... exports. Never done a day's work in their bloody lives ... He gets up and goes round to every table.

MRS BURNETT. What?

SHAW. 'I'd like you to know,' he says, 'that *that* lady and *that* gentleman, sitting over there, is – my mother and – my dad. The finest mother and the finest father you ever saw.'

MRS BURNETT. He said that?

SHAW. At every table. Went round the entire place.

MRS SHAW. He did. I didn't know where to put myself.

SHAW. 'If you'd like to do something which, in years to come, you'll be able to recount to your grandchildren, with pride, with a feeling of achievement, then get up, off your backsides, go over there, and shake them by the hand.'

MRS BURNETT. He did that?

MRS SHAW. I thought they'd throw us out.

SHAW. Throw us out? ... They couldn't afford it. (*Indicating* COLIN) Tipped the waiter two fivers when we went in ...

MRS SHAW. Head-waiter ...

SHAW. Head-waiter. 'Keep an eye on us, will you?' An eye! For that I'd have kept both bloody feet and half a dozen hands.

(*They laugh.*)

MRS SHAW. Now, now. Just go careful. (*To* MRS BURNETT) He hasn't been very discreet with some of his jokes.

SHAW. Nay, when I have a good time I have one. No shilly-shallying about. I know how to enjoy myself, I do.

REARDON. That's right. I can vouch for it now. As long as I care
to remember.

ANDREW. A toast then ...

COLIN. A toast ...

ANDREW. Are you totted up, Steve?

STEVEN. Yes. I'm fine.

ANDREW. To the finest mother and the finest dad that these
three sons have ever had.
(*They laugh.*)
To the finest mother and the finest dad.

ALL (*but* MRS SHAW). To the finest mother and the finest dad.
(*They drink.*)

ANDREW (*to* SHAW). Nay, you don't say it, you daft nut.

SHAW. What ... ? (*They laugh.*)

COLIN. It's you we're toasting.

REARDON. Never lost the opportunity to take a glass.

SHAW. No. He's right. I never have ... To the best wife, my
darling, in the land.

REARDON. Aye.

SHAW. The best wife that any man could have.

ALL. The best wife!
(*They drink.*)

REARDON. To the best family in the land.

ALL. The best family in the land.
(*They drink.*)

SHAW. To the best neighbours that a man could wish to have.

ALL. The best neighbours!
(*They drink.*)

SHAW. I've damn well run out.

REARDON. Now, then. Allow me, if you don't mind, to put that
immediately to rights. (*Offers bottle round.*)

MRS BURNETT. No, no. I think I've had enough.

STEVEN. No, no. I'm all right.
(*The others take a refill.* MRS SHAW *shakes her head.*)

63

SHAW. We'll soon get through this. Come this time tomorrow …

REARDON. Plenty more where this came from, I'm thinking.

SHAW. Aye. Aye. The sky's the limit!

REARDON. Like the old days, Harry.

SHAW. Like the old days, Jim. You're right. There wasn't a bar we didn't turn upside down in those days.

MRS SHAW. The terror of the town.

SHAW. We were. We were … Didn't know Jim here was once a professional fighter.

STEVEN. No.

ANDREW. I don't believe I did.

REARDON. For four consecutive weeks it lasted.

>   (*They laugh.*)

SHAW. Jim's trouble – shall I tell you? … Never done a day's hard work in all his bloody life. Licking envelopes, filling in forms, wage-packets: dangling round the manager's back pocket.

REARDON. Ah, now, any damn fool can wield a pick and shovel. Takes a man with brains to get paid for sitting on his backside. Ask your sons, Harry.

SHAW. He's right. He's right. I'll tell you something now … Do you know how high it is where I work?

>   (*He looks round.*
>   *They shake their heads.*)

SHAW. Thirteen inches.

COLIN. It can't be.

SHAW. Thirteen inches. (*Stoops and measures it off the floor with his hand.*)

REARDON. He's right. The Rawcliffe seam.

SHAW. Thirteen inches. If I as much as cough, the whole damn roof'll come down on top of me. Two hundred yards of rock above, and the centre of the earth beneath. Why, you're nothing but a piece of stone yourself, propped up between one bit and the next. You lie with your belly shoved up against your throat.

MRS SHAW. Oh, now. We've just had our dinner ...

SHAW. They don't believe me, you know. I've often thought I ought to take her down, just once, in all these years, for her to see what it's like.

MRS SHAW. I've heard enough, without having to find out.

SHAW. Nay, you can't know what it's like unless you've been down ... And not even then. It takes a few years of going down before you get a glimmer ... You get a view of life you don't get anywhere else. You really get a feeling of what God's good protection means. (*Coughs*) I tell you, if you stuck a pin in me you wouldn't get any blood: a little pile of coal-dust'd be all you'd see run out.

(*They laugh.*)

MRS SHAW. He ought to come out. While he's got two arms, and two legs. And a head to go with it.

SHAW. Nay, they don't understand. You have some pride. Damn it all. You can't just come out and leave it. What's it all add up to?

MRS SHAW. Fifty years of good fortune. How many men have you seen maimed? And killed.

SHAW. Aye. Well. I shan't get morbid. Not at this hour of the night. Mrs Burnett: another drop!

MRS BURNETT. I ought to be going ... One last one, then.

REARDON. She has a great gift for it, I saw it at a glance.

MRS BURNETT. Once at Christmas. That's the only time I try ... and on an occasion like this, of course.

REARDON. My dear lady ... (*Fills her glass*) Steven: Your father tells me you have a learned text on the way as well.

STEVEN. Had. It's on the way, I'm afraid, no longer.

REARDON. Ah, now, artistic endeavour. It's open to a great many disappointments.

STEVEN. Well, it was nothing as ambitious as that.

REARDON. And what was your subject, Steven? If you don't mind me asking.

STEVEN. I'm not sure myself.

ANDREW. It was a summing up, Mr Reardon, of society as it is today.

REARDON. Society today? And is society today any different from society yesterday?

STEVEN. I suspect not. In any case ...

REARDON (*encouraging*). No, no. Despite appearances to the contrary, I have a student's curiosity about the world. How it came to be; what it is; and in what manner it will die out.

MRS BURNETT. Believes we're going to be bombed to death. Going to build himself a shelter.

REARDON. Well, well. A figure of speech.

MRS BURNETT. No, no. He said a shelter. Wanted me to come in it with him.

ANDREW. Mr Reardon!

MRS SHAW. Where? Not round here, I hope.

REARDON. No. No. A figure of speech. A figure of speech entirely.

SHAW. Do you remember the shelters during the war, then, Jim?

REARDON. Do I not? ... A certain one I recollect of a remarkable construction. (*To the others*) The largest hole you ever saw.

SHAW. These lads: they won't remember it.

ANDREW. Remember it? We dug the bloody thing.

SHAW. Went down ... what was it? Fourteen feet. (*To* MRS BURNETT) Should have seen it.

ANDREW. You're forgetting, now. She did.

SHAW. 'Course. 'Course. Forgetting. Opened it first night of bombing to let her in ... Swam around, then, didn't you, love?

MRS BURNETT. I nearly drowned! Calls himself a miner ...

SHAW. Nay, ladies first. Alus been my motto ... (*Laughs*) Whole place was full of water ... By go ... Freetened of being bombed to death and you end up being drowned. (*Laughs*.)

(MRS SHAW *has begun to hum the hymn tune 'Aberystwyth'
quietly to herself.*)

REARDON. It was truly a miner's work of art. But for the fact
that it was always full of water, it would have been of in-
calculable benefit to us all. As it was ...

MRS BURNETT. Spent all the time in the cupboard underneath
the stairs.

REARDON. We did. Many a happy hour have I spent playing
cards by the light of a single candle while the drone of
German bombers came, hour after hour, from overhead.

SHAW. I used to carry Steven out. To watch the rockets. They
came over sometimes in threes.

REARDON. I remember.

SHAW. You could see the flames from their exhausts ... used to
rattle ... (*Indicating* STEVEN) He took it all to heart. Tried to
tell him – you could tell when they were going to land ...
Engines cut out. Silent ... Hell of an explosion.

REARDON (*to* MRS BURNETT). No warning, now, the next time.
Liquefaction will be the order of the day.

SHAW. Aye. It doesn't bear thinking of.

REARDON. No. No. Thank God we've reached the twilight.

SHAW. In one piece.

REARDON. In one piece. You're right.

    (*They're silent.*

    MRS SHAW *humming, then at the third line:*)

MRS SHAW (*sings quietly*).

       While the tempest still is high:

       Hide me, O my Saviour, hide,

       Till the storm of life is past;

       Safe into the haven guide,

       O receive my soul at last.

    (COLIN, ANDREW *and* STEVEN *exchange looks,* ANDREW
turning away to hide his laugh.)

MRS SHAW (*sings*). Other refuge have I none ...

(REARDON *starts, then* SHAW, *to sing too.*)
> Hangs my helpless soul on Thee;
> Leave, ah! Leave me not alone,
> Still support and comfort me ...

(MRS BURNETT *has started to sing too, they sing strongly.*
At the last ANDREW, *then* COLIN *and* STEVEN, *join in.*)
> All my trust on Thee is stay'd,
> All my help from Thee I bring;
> Cover my defenceless head
> With the shadow of Thy wing.

(MRS SHAW *carries on humming the tune.*)

COLIN (*to* ANDREW). Remember Sunday School?

ANDREW. 'Crusaders'. I was in 'St Andrew's', appropriately enough ... He was in 'St Peter's' ... each saint, you see, had a different pew.

COLIN. A different banner to each group.

ANDREW. St Peter was a fish. Eye-balls like damn great saucers.

COLIN. St Francis a bird ...

ANDREW. One leg, and a beak like a damn great parrot.

COLIN. He was no artist, that's for sure, who painted those.

ANDREW. No ... Jamey, now. He'd have gone down like a bomb.

COLIN. Jamey ...

MRS BURNETT. He would. (*To* REARDON) We were just saying earlier on ...

SHAW (*to* REARDON). Do you remember the night he died?

REARDON. I do. I shall never forget ...

SHAW (*indicating* REARDON). Woke him up ... knocking at his door.

REARDON. Aye ... he did.

SHAW. We were just lying there in bed ... couldn't sleep ... could we, love? ... then suddenly on the wall, just above the bed, three damn great crashes ... Like a fist ...

MRS SHAW. Bigger ...

SHAW. Bigger. Like a damn great giant ... Shook the house ...

Tell you, frightened us to bloody death. Went to Jim's ... he sat with us ...

REARDON. The rest of the night.

SHAW. I've never been able to make that out. There were you two ... (*Indicating* COLIN *and* ANDREW) Never heard it ...

MRS SHAW. Slept right through ...

SHAW. I could never make that out. Three blows. Just like that ... The only two who heard it. (*Indicating himself and* MRS SHAW. *To* ANDREW) He died, you know, without any warning ... caught a chill one night ... dead by the next morning. Couldn't believe it ... I'd have given aught to have saved that lad ... Asked Him a time or two to take me in his place ... willed them rocks, I have, to fall on my bloody head ... He was a lovely lad ... I'd have given bloody aught. Still. (*Sees* MRS SHAW's *look*) Aye. Well, then ...

MRS SHAW. I shall have to go to bed. I'm sorry. But I'm nearly asleep sitting here ... All this excitement.

MRS BURNETT. Aye. Look at the time ... I only came across to make up the fire. I've left the light on, the door open.

SHAW. Never mind, love. A damn good job you made of it.

REARDON. Shall I escort you across the way?

MRS BURNETT. No, no, I'll manage on my own, if you don't mind. I'll see you all tomorrow. (*To* MRS SHAW) I'm glad you've had a good night, love.

MRS SHAW. Yes. Thanks, love. I'll see you tomorrow ... all being well.

MRS BURNETT. All being well. Sleep tight ... I'll let myself out. (*She goes.*)

REARDON. Ah, well. I better be off, too. My wife will be thinking I've run away at last. After all these years, now, I don't wish to raise her hopes unduly.

MRS SHAW. Oh, now. Get on ... (*He goes to the door.*)

REARDON. I shall pop in, if I may, in the morning, and say my farewells.

ANDREW. Aye. We'll have one more before we go.

REARDON. Now there's a promise I'll not forget ... Good night.
And may sweet dreams illuminate your slumbers.

    (*They laugh, call 'good night', and he goes.*)

MRS SHAW (*cheerful*). It's been a lovely night. It has ... But if I
stay up any longer ... Do you know where you're all sleeping?

COLIN. Don't worry. We'll toss up ... Good night, Mother.
God bless ... (*Embracing her.*)

MRS SHAW. Good night, love ... it's been a lovely night, it has ...

    (*To* STEVEN) Good night, love ...

    (*To* ANDREW) Good night, love ...

    (*They kiss her cheek in turn.*)

    See you in the morning ... You don't mind me going off?

COLIN. No. No. You get your rest.

SHAW. I'll be up in a jiffy, love. Shan't be long.

MRS SHAW. Good night, then. And thank you all again.

COLIN, ANDREW. Good night ...

    (*She goes.*)

SHAW. Aye ... She's enjoyed tonight. She has ... Wouldn't have
sung that hymn if she hadn't! (*They laugh. To* COLIN) Nay,
you take it from me, lad. That's the best night she's ever had ...

ANDREW (*to* COLIN). Heads I sleep upstairs, tails you sleep down
here.

COLIN. Right ...

    (ANDREW *tosses a coin.*)

ANDREW. Tails ... You sleep down here ... (*To* STEVEN) Heads
I sleep up, tails you sleep down ...

COLIN. Ay ... wait a minute!

    (*They laugh.*)

ANDREW. The destiny of fifteen thousand men rests in his hands,
and you can fiddle him with a penny.

    (*They laugh,* SHAW *turning to the mantelpiece, and taking
down a box of matches.*)

COLIN. It's late. That's the only reason.

ANDREW. God bless our motor industry, and all who crucify themselves inside her.

SHAW. Here. Shortest match sleeps down. (*Holds three between his fingers, the ends concealed*) ... Steve ...

STEVEN (*takes one*). Not me.

COLIN. (*takes one*) ... Me.
(*They laugh.*)

STEVEN. Ah, bad luck.

ANDREW. I hope, for the nation's sake, you have better luck at work.

COLIN. Oh, it won't be so bad. (*Trying the settee*) Fine.

SHAW. Ah, well. A damn fine night. You can have it all. A car money, a big house ... They're nowt. A family like this That's all that counts.

ANDREW. You can tell he's enjoyed himself.

SHAW. I have. I have. Tonight's meant more to me than owt.
(COLIN *yawns, stretches.*)
Ah, well. I'll leave you to it ... this time tomorrow I'll be back down. Nights ... It's one I'll remember. I want you to know that. You've made me and your mother very proud.

COLIN ... Nothing of it. We'll be back again this time next year, don't worry.

SHAW. Nay, I might damn well hold you to that as well ... Good night. And God bless you ... (*To* STEVEN *as he passes* SHAW *on the way to the stairs*) You're coming up?

STEVEN. Aye ...
(STEVEN *goes.*)

SHAW (*watches him, then*). Is Steve all right?

COLIN. What?

SHAW. I don't know ... He's not looked very well.

COLIN. Oh, he's all right ... (*Looks to* ANDREW.)

ANDREW. Aye.

SHAW. He works too hard. He's always put too much into whatever he did.

COLIN. He'll be all right.

SHAW. Aye. Right. Well ... I'll get off. Good night again.

COLIN. Good night, Dad.

ANDREW. Good night.

SHAW. Don't make a noise, will you? Your mother sleeps very light ... Good night.

(*He goes.*)

ANDREW. A fiver.

COLIN (*pause*). What?

ANDREW. Me bed.

COLIN. You're joking.

ANDREW. I'm not. (*Feels the sofa*) Ugh. Iron. They've had this twenty years.

COLIN. They haven't. I bought it for them only last year.

ANDREW. Terrible taste.

COLIN. It was their taste. My money. I'm not going to tell them what to buy.

ANDREW. Rest of the furniture, too?

COLIN. Just about.

ANDREW. What about it?

COLIN. Not likely.

ANDREW. You stingy sod. The money you earn, no dependents. And you won't give up five quid for a decent bed.

COLIN. It's not that. It's just a feeling of repugnance.

ANDREW. Repugnance?

COLIN. My brother selling me his bed – well, not even his – for five pounds.

ANDREW. Course, you could go in the car. But then ... you might get run over.

COLIN. Or back to 'The Excelsior'. Don't worry. I know your mentality. The fact is, for me, it's a privilege sleeping in this house.

ANDREW. A privilege? Here ... are you all right?

COLIN. Look. I honour what my mother and father have done.

And I don't give a sod for your bloody family analysis ...

ANDREW. Four pounds ten.

COLIN. No.

ANDREW. All right. A sacrifice. Four.

COLIN. Nothing. I'm sleeping here.

ANDREW (*watching him*). High-pressure meetings tomorrow morning.

COLIN. I have, as a matter of fact. Tomorrow afternoon.

ANDREW. I don't know how they've managed without you. (*Looks at the clock*) Must be what? ... ten hours since they last saw you ... You're not getting undressed, are you?

COLIN. Not entirely. No. (*Begins to take off his shoes, jacket and waistcoat.*)

ANDREW. You know. I just can't make this out ... Only two years ago, it seems, you were running in through that door with little short trousers and a snotty nose.

COLIN. I'm tired. I've got to drive back and work tomorrow.

ANDREW. Yes, well. You're a busy man ... I suppose you have a secretarial assistant.

COLIN. Yes ...

ANDREW. Don't you ever ... you know, feel you could make some progress with her?

COLIN. She happens to be a man.

ANDREW. A man!

COLIN. The assistance I require is not the kind that you imagine. There are any amount of women pushing typewriters.

ANDREW. I see ... On second thoughts, I might be safer upstairs.

COLIN. Good. I'm glad. Good night.

ANDREW. Shall I put out the light?

COLIN. If you don't mind. I'll be very grateful.

ANDREW. And ... er ... I won't say anything to Mum.

COLIN. Look. Hop it. Scarper. Knock off.

ANDREW. I'm going ...

(*Puts out the light; goes.* COLIN *settles on the settee beneath a blanket.*

A moment later ANDREW *reappears.*)

COLIN. Is anything the matter?

ANDREW. Forgot to say good night.

COLIN. *Good night!*

ANDREW. Three quid.

COLIN. *Good night!*

ANDREW. Two.

COLIN. *Good night!*

ANDREW. Ah, well. I hope it kills you ... (*Goes: comes back in*) I hope, when you come to negotiate tomorrow afternoon, you can't even *sit down*!

COLIN. Good.

ANDREW. One pound ten.

COLIN. For Christ's sake!

ANDREW. Right ... I'm going.

(ANDREW *goes.*

COLIN *settles down again, turns one way then another, settles down.*

After a while ANDREW *comes back, in shirt sleeves.*)

ANDREW. Psst ...

COLIN. Wha ...

ANDREW. Are you asleep?

COLIN. For Christ's sake.

(ANDREW *puts on the light.*)

COLIN. Oh! ... God! (*Shields his eyes, half-rising.*)

ANDREW. It's Steven.

COLIN. What ... ?

ANDREW. He's at it again.

COLIN. What ... ?

ANDREW. Crying.

COLIN. Oh, Christ.

ANDREW. In his sleep.

COLIN. Oh, God ... (*Gets up*) What's the matter with him.

ANDREW. How do I know?

COLIN. Can't you wake him?

ANDREW. I don't know ... All right. I suppose I'll have to.

COLIN. Look ... He may have drunk too much.

ANDREW. You must be joking.

COLIN. It could be anything. Indigestion ...

ANDREW. Indigestion?

COLIN. Anything ...

ANDREW. All right. You go. If you're so bloody efficient. (*Sits down on settee*) Perhaps you can negotiate some suitable compromise ... Let's say ... a whimper.

COLIN (*goes to stair*). I can't hear anything ...

ANDREW. No. Probably not.

COLIN. Look. Is this something you've just ... What're you doing?

ANDREW. Well, I can't sleep up there with that row going on. (*He's taken* COLIN's *place on the settee, lying down.*) It's yours. For nothing.

COLIN. Look here ... God. There's somebody getting up. (*Listens at the door.*)

ANDREW. It'll be Steven ...

COLIN. No ... (*Listens*) My dad ... Oh, Christ.

ANDREW. Better go up.

(COLIN *listens at the door leading to the stairs*)
It's not so bad here after all. I was wrong ... (*Eases himself, covering himself more surely with the blanket*) ... Bit more on the fire, and we'll be all right.

COLIN. Oh, Christ.

ANDREW. What?

COLIN (*coming across*). He's coming down.

ANDREW. Better get the cards out. Be here all night ... Where's that Scotch?

COLIN. Look, you better get up off there ...

SHAW (*coming in, blindly, in trousers and shirt*). What's going on, then?

ANDREW. What ... Colin's just off to bed. I've swapped him. Need a spot of oil. Hear those springs? Christ ...

SHAW. There's Steven ...

ANDREW. Steven? (*Looks around.*)

SHAW. Upstairs, in bed.

ANDREW. What ... ?

SHAW. I've just been in.

ANDREW. Sleeping. Wind ...

SHAW. Well ... I've never heard a noise like it ...

ANDREW (*matter-of-fact*). Look here, Col. You better go up and have a look.

COLIN. What ... ?

ANDREW (*getting up*). All right. I'll go. (*To* SHAW) What did he say?

SHAW. Nothing ...

ANDREW. Right ... Well. (*Nods at* COLIN) Soon settle that. Can't have him saying nothing ... Right ... Well ... Off we go. (*Looks round then goes.*)

COLIN. Do you fancy another drink?

SHAW. I couldn't touch another. I couldn't ... I was ... look. I was fast asleep and I thought it was a cat. Then I thought it was in here ... then ... (*Listens*) I don't know ... If your mother hears ... I've shut her door.

COLIN. He could be just dreaming.

SHAW. He was awake. His eyes were open. When I leaned over him he shook his head. (*Looks up. Listens*) He never cried as a baby ... Did you know that? ... The only time he ever cried was once ... I better go up.

COLIN. Right ... look ... All right. No. Look ... We'll both go up ...

SHAW. Don't make a noise ...

(SHAW *has gone to the door: as he goes out, and* COLIN *makes to follow him, he pauses.*)

Oh ... He's coming ...

(SHAW *comes back in.*)

He's coming ...

COLIN. Who?

(ANDREW *comes in.*)

SHAW. What's he say?

ANDREW. Dreaming ... nothing ... right as rain. (*Looks round*) Better have another drop. Knock us all out together.

SHAW. He's been working too damned hard. I know. I could see it when he first came. He's always been so conscientious.

ANDREW. He's coming down ... Dressing-gown. Would you believe it? Brought it in his little bag ... Show you he's all right. Dreaming. Wind. Nothing to worry about. (*To* COLIN) That *steak Diane* ... I almost made a complaint when I first saw it. Did you see him put it in the pan?

COLIN. No ...

ANDREW. Damn faded colour. Set light to it before you could have a proper look. Chopped onions and mushrooms on top of it ... I bet they'd had that in for weeks waiting for somebody like us ... uneducated. Inexperienced.

(SHAW *is looking towards the stairs.*)

ANDREW. What was yours?

COLIN. Tartare ... Steak.

ANDREW. I'd have thought that was very fresh ... Going by the colour. Blood red.

COLIN. Yes ...

(STEVEN *has appeared. He's wearing a dressing-gown, his trousers underneath.*)

ANDREW. Steve's was the rump, wasn't it?

COLIN. Sirloin ...

ANDREW. Sirloin ... Could easily have been that. I wouldn't have minded having another look at those carrots. The way he served them from the pot ...

COLIN (*holding his stomach*). All right ...

> (STEVEN *has sat down.*)

SHAW. Are you all right, Steve?

STEVEN. Yes.

SHAW. I mean, nay lad ... if there's anything the matter.

STEVEN. No.

SHAW. It's not Sheila is it?

STEVEN. No. No. (*Shakes his head.*)

ANDREW. Sirloin ... If we'd all had steak tartare like Colin ... trust him him to have all the luck.

SHAW. Nay, look ... I don't know ... Your mother'd be that unhappy to see you upset ...

ANDREW. She would.

SHAW. You're not ill? ... I mean ...

STEVEN. No ... (*He shakes his head.*)

SHAW. Well ... It could be tonight ... All that excitement. I mean, well, it's been a very emotional evening for all of us.

COLIN. It has ... What with that.

ANDREW ... And the *steak Diane*.

COLIN (*to* ANDREW). Look. I think we've had enough.

ANDREW. Yes. (*Walks about, hands in pockets, whistling quietly to himself.*

> STEVEN *sits as if abstracted.*
>
> *To* COLIN.)

Better watch it.

COLIN. What?

ANDREW. Watch it.

COLIN. Look. I've just about had enough ... His systematic ... bloody ... disparagement ... of every ... bleeding thing ... inside this house ...

SHAW. I don't know what's going on, you know, but you better keep your voices down. I'm not having your mother woken

up. If you have any arguments you can save them till tomorrow ... outside, any time. But not down here. I've asked
you that.

ANDREW. Why not? What's she to be protected from?

SHAW. What?

ANDREW. I mean ... that ... Goddess, we have up there.

SHAW. What?

COLIN (*to* SHAW). Take no notice of him. He's drunk. He
doesn't know what he's saying.

ANDREW. He'd know of course. The supreme bloody sycophant.
The professional bloody paster-over-er. The smoother-
downer. The shoddy, fifth-rate, sycophantic whore ...

SHAW. Look ... look ... you better get out ...

ANDREW. Get out? I've never been in.

SHAW. What ... ?

ANDREW. This family.

COLIN. Oh God.

SHAW. What ... ?

ANDREW. Look. (*Points to* STEVEN.) Tears! What the hell is he
crying for?

COLIN. You better get out. Go on. I'll bloody turn you out
myself.

ANDREW. Dad. Wise up. You've enshrined that woman in so
much adoration that she's well-nigh invisible to you as well
as to everybody else.

SHAW. What ... ?

ANDREW. You owe her *nothing*. What're you trying to pay off?

SHAW. What ... ?

(SHAW *stands, blinded, in the centre of the room.*)

COLIN (*to* ANDREW). I think you better go. Go on. I'll give you
the keys. You can drive to the hotel.

ANDREW. I've no money on me.

COLIN. ... (*Hunts round for his coat.*)

ANDREW. Aye ... Aye ... (*Watches* COLIN *get the notes out. Then, as he offers them*) Are you actually aware ... I mean, of what you're doing?

COLIN. I am.

ANDREW. I mean, can you actually detach yourself a moment – perverse as such an action well might be – and actually see what it is you're doing?

COLIN. I'm protecting ...

ANDREW. Protecting? You're protecting nothing. (*To* SHAW) He's the one you ought to kick out. And that one with him. up yonder ... The one that's made us so bloody clean and whole.

SHAW. What ... ?

COLIN (*to* SHAW). Leave him. It's envy. It's jealousy. Listen to nothing he has to say.

ANDREW. No, no. He's right. Listen to nothing that I have to say. Instead ... (*Gestures at* STEVEN) Fasten your eyes on that.

SHAW. If ... What ... ? (*Holds his head.*)

COLIN. Dad ... (*Takes* SHAW's *shoulder.*)

ANDREW. Come on, Steve. You're not deaf. You've heard it. What is it, seething around inside that head, that causes you and ... *look* ... my dad, to cry?

  (STEVEN *stands up. He gazes before him a moment, distracted.*)
No, no. No rush. No hurry. Come on ... What's eating out your mind?

COLIN. Shut up.

STEVEN. I've ... (*Shakes his head.*)

SHAW. Look ... Steve ...

  (SHAW *goes to* STEVEN. *He puts his arm round him, as much for his own support as* STEVEN's.)
You mustn't lad ... You mustn't ... Nay. All I ever had ...

COLIN (*to* ANDREW). God. I'll bloody kill you for this.

SHAW. Nay ... every night ... Look, Steve ...

ANDREW. I hope she's listening. (*Looks up*) I hope you're listening ... I hope in all sincerity she can hear ... Her sons, her abject bloody lover ... commend their bloody souls to thee.

COLIN. For Christ's sake.

(SHAW *has turned away, lost.*)

ANDREW. Dad. Dad. Forty years ... what chance have we ever had with *that*! ... Steve ... Steve ... Tell him.

COLIN. I'll bloody kill you for this! I will! I'll bloody kill you!

ANDREW. Let's negotiate a settlement, Col ... Forty years of my father's life for a lady like my mother, conscientious, devout of temperament, overtly religious ... sincere ... for getting her with child at the age of eighteen, nineteen, twenty ... I've forgotten which ... on the back of which imprudence we have been borne all our lives, labouring to atone for her sexuality ... labouring to atone for ... what? Labouring to atone ... When I think of all the books I've had to read. When I think of all the facts I've had to learn. The texts I've had to study. The exams I've had to ... with that vision held perpetually before me; a home, a car, a wife ... a child ... a rug that didn't have holes in, a pocket that never leaked ... I even married a Rector's daughter! For Christ's sake: how *good* could I become? The edifice of my life – of *his* life – built up on that ... We – *we* – are the inheritors of nothing ... totems ... while all the time the Godhead ... slumbers overhead.

STEVEN. My mother ...

ANDREW. What?

(STEVEN *has shaken his head.*)

COLIN. You blame them for that ... ?

ANDREW. Blame? Blame? ... Blame ... Good God. No blame. No bloody nothing.

STEVEN. No ... (*He shakes his head*) No.

ANDREW. ... What is it, Dad? What image did you have ... crawling around down there at night ... panting, bleeding, blackened ... What world was it you were hoping we'd inherit?

COLIN. Shurrup. For Christ's sake, shurrup.

ANDREW. These aren't your sons, old man ... I don't know what you see here ... But these are nothing ... less than nothing ... has-beens, wash-outs, semblances ... a pathetic vision of a better life ...

COLIN. I think you've said enough.

ANDREW. Enough? Life measured out in motor-cars ... I'll put one on your tomb ... I hope tomorrow you have a damn great strike. And I hope they come along and ask you to negotiate. I hope they make you Chancellor, or Prime Minister. And I hope it gives you something to do, fills in your time, infects your life with a certain feeling of significance and meaning ... for if it doesn't, I hold out for you, Colin, *brother*, no hope of any kind at all.

Steve? ... (*No answer*) ... Dad? ... Fast asleep ...

(SHAW *sits dazed across the room.*)

Why not ... Steve? ... Nothing. I'll go on up, then. Cheerio.
(*He goes to the stairs, and goes.*)

COLIN. My God ...

(*They're silent for a moment*)

Dad? ... It's all right ...

(*He goes across to him*)

Dad?

SHAW. Aye ...

COLIN. It's all right ... It's all right.

SHAW. Aye ...

COLIN. Are you listening? ... Dad!

SHAW. Aye ... It's ... (*Shakes his head.*)

COLIN. Look. It's okay ... Are you listening?

SHAW. Nay ... whatever's happened? ... I don't know.

STEVEN. Dad?

SHAW. I'd do owt for you lads. You know that.

COLIN. Aye. We do.

SHAW. I don't know ...

COLIN. Trust the Shaws ... Not two minutes together – and out it comes ... Fists all over the place.

SHAW. I'll never forgive him for that. You know. I won't ...

STEVEN. Dad ... Don't.

SHAW. Nay, lad. He took advantage of us ... If your mother ever got to hear, it'd tear her in two.

STEVEN. Dad ... Leave it.

SHAW. Aye ... I know. You do too much, Steven. You've got to live your life as well as work. There's Sheila. Your family ... I can tell you, I know what too much work does to a man.

STEVEN. Yes ... Well, Dad ... You go to bed.

SHAW. I could sleep down here ...

STEVEN. Now what for? ... You go up. Go on ... No. Look. I'm all right ...

SHAW. Nay ... I don't know ... Are you going up?

STEVEN. I am. In a minute ... Go on ...

SHAW. I shouldn't sleep with him up yonder.

STEVEN. Dad: he was upset as well ...

SHAW. I should stay with Colin. Let him lie up there alone.

STEVEN. Go on, now ... you get off.

COLIN. Aye ... Go on, Dad. We'll be all right.

SHAW. I hope to God she's not awake ...

COLIN. She won't be. Don't worry.

SHAW. In the morning ...

COLIN. Don't worry. We'll have that troublemaker out.

SHAW. Aye ... Right ... He said some things ...

COLIN. Go on, now ...

SHAW. Aye. Well ... Good night, lads.

COLIN. Good night, Dad.

SHAW. Aye ... Well ... Good night ...

(*He turns and goes.*)

COLIN (*sighs; then, to* STEVEN). Do you want a drink?

STEVEN. No ... (*Shakes his head.*)

COLIN. I'll have one. I'll have two, I think. (*He's gone to pour it out*.) Christ. Thanks for small mercies ... (STEVEN *looks up*) My dad. Didn't understand a word.

STEVEN. No ... He's like a child.

COLIN. Andrew? ... Say that again.

(COLIN *watches* STEVEN *for a while, uncertain of his mood. Then:*)

STEVEN. The funny thing is ... (*he laughs*) The funny thing is that he (*gestures up*) raised us to better things which, in his heart – my dad – he despises even more than Andrew ... I mean, his work actually has significance for him ... while the work he's educated us to do ... is nothing ... at the best a pastime, at the worst a sort of soulless stirring of the pot ... Honestly, what hope have any of us got?

COLIN. I think I'll have another.

STEVEN. What actually do you do with it, Colin?

COLIN. What ...

STEVEN. I mean, this feeling of disfigurement.

COLIN. Disfigurement?

STEVEN. I mean ... this crushing, bloody sense of injury ... inflicted, as he says, by wholly innocent hands.

COLIN. Well, I don't ...

STEVEN. No. Well ... I better get up.

COLIN. Do you ... I mean, have you had any medical advice?

STEVEN. Advice?

COLIN. About your ...

STEVEN. No ... Well ...

COLIN. Shouldn't you get some sort of guidance? I mean, Christ, there's any amount of stuff nowadays.

STEVEN. Yep ...

COLIN. Christ, if we all thought like that maniac up yonder – we'd all be what?

STEVEN. Artists, most likely.

COLIN. Sure. (*Laughs*) And I can just see the sort of art ...

STEVEN. Aye. Well, I better get up.

COLIN. First thing in the morning – we must get him out.

STEVEN. Yep ... Right ... I'll say good night.

COLIN. Are you okay, then ... ?

STEVEN. Sure ... Right ... I'll see you.

COLIN. Good night, Steve, then ...

STEVEN. Aye ... Good night.

(STEVEN *goes.*

COLIN *gazes after him a moment; then he glances round. He picks up the blanket, the glass, puts out the light. He goes to sit in a chair by the fire, wraps the blanket about him. He drinks from the glass, empties it, then sits gazing at the fire.*)

SLOW FADE

Scene 2

Morning.

COLIN *is sleeping in the chair, his head fallen on one side. There's the sound of activity in the kitchen, plates, cups, etc.*

After a moment MRS SHAW *comes in, dressed, from the kitchen. She goes to the window, opens the curtains.*

COLIN. Oh ... Oh! ... (*Eases himself stiffly in the chair, wakening.*)

MRS SHAW. Did I wake you, love? I've made the breakfast ... If we don't eat it it'll all get cold.

COLIN. Yes ... Aye. (*Stretches.*)

MRS SHAW. Did you sleep all right?

COLIN. Yes. Fine ...

MRS SHAW. What was the matter with the couch?

COLIN. Oh ... I ... dropped off here.

MRS SHAW. I thought it'd be either you or Steven. Trust Andrew. Snoring his head off in bed.

COLIN. Aye. (*Rubs his hair. Gets up. Stretches his stiff body.*)

MRS SHAW. Fire's still going from last night. We were up that late. What time do you have to be leaving?

COLIN. Oh, pretty soon. Straight after breakfast ... Sleep all right?

MRS SHAW. Like a top. It was a lovely night. Thank you. (*Kisses his cheek in passing*) I'll just fetch it through. (*Goes.*)

COLIN (*looks out of the window*). Rain ... Looks like it.

MRS SHAW (*off*). We don't get much else this time of the year.

COLIN (*talking through*). You know, you ought to get my dad to retire. He'll listen to you. Not to us ... I can get you a house on the coast, a cottage or a bungalow. You'd have no extra work to do.

MRS SHAW (*re-entering with the tray*). Nay, I've tried. Work for your father, well, it's something he doesn't seem able to do without.

COLIN. Even then, I think you could persuade him. There must be some inducement he'll listen to.

MRS SHAW. He's not going to come out of that pit until they carry him out, and then he'd go back at the first chance. I don't know ... He's been a good man. But I don't know: in some things he's been very simple.

COLIN. Aye ... (*Turns away and starts to get dressed, i.e. tie, waistcoat, shoes, jacket.*)

MRS SHAW. I'll go and call them down. Andrew'll sleep all day, if I remember.

COLIN. Aye ...

    (*She goes.*)

MRS SHAW (*off*). Dad ... Steven!

SHAW (*off*). I'm coming.

MRS SHAW (*off*). Can you knock up the others? Tell them it's getting cold.

SHAW (*off*). Aye ... Aye ... I will.

MRS SHAW (*reappearing*). Well, then. That's that ... What time do you want to be off by?

COLIN. Oh, as soon as that one up there is ready.

MRS SHAW. Are you taking him back with you?

COLIN. I suppose I'll have to.

MRS SHAW. He's wrecking his career. I suppose you realize that? ... Still. They're old enough to look after their own affairs at his age ... He was always wild.

COLIN. Yes ...

MRS SHAW. I don't know. He took it very badly ...

COLIN. What? ...

MRS SHAW. When Jamey died. He was five years old – Andrew. We put him out with Mr Reardon, you know, when Steven was born.

COLIN. Why was that?

MRS SHAW. Nay, love. To save me the work ... Saved my life, you did, you know. We kept you at home. You were only two. (*Kisses his head*) I don't know where we'd have been without ... I don't think he's ever forgiven me.

COLIN. What? ...

MRS SHAW. Andrew ... He was away six weeks. He used to come to the door, crying, you know. I don't know ... I tried to tell him. If he'd have been here we'd have had a terrible time. What with your dad at work, Steven ... Jamey ...

COLIN. Aye, well. We all have our problems, love.

MRS SHAW. We have ... As you get older you find more and more that these things somehow work out.

COLIN. Aye. That's right ...

MRS SHAW (*she goes to the stairs. Calls*). Dad! It's getting cold ... I'll have to tip it away in a minute.

SHAW (*off*). Aye ... We're coming.

MRS SHAW (*to* COLIN). Well, we better be getting ours.

COLIN. Yes.

MRS SHAW. And how's your work going?

COLIN. Oh. Very well ... As a matter of fact ...

MRS SHAW. Yes ...

COLIN. Well, I didn't want to tell you about it ... until I was more certain ...

MRS SHAW. Now ... you'll have to. Come on ...

COLIN. Nay, well ... (*Scratches his head.*)

MRS SHAW. Come on. We'll have it out of you ...

COLIN. Well, it's not finally settled ... But fairly soon, now ...

MRS SHAW. Come on!

COLIN. I might be getting married.

MRS SHAW. Well!

COLIN. It's not all been agreed yet. But it's ... sort of on the cards.

MRS SHAW. Well!

COLIN. So ...

MRS SHAW. Here. Let me give you a kiss, love. (*She comes round the table and kisses his cheek*) Well, then ... Congratulations ... I knew something was up!

COLIN. Up?

MRS SHAW. Oh, your mood. I could tell. On top of things ... Well, then. And what's she do?

COLIN. A dentist.

MRS SHAW. A dentist!

COLIN. I'll bring her up ... You can have a look. Better still – you can come down. Show you round the factory.

MRS SHAW. Well, then ... (*Watches him, pleased*) Have you told your dad?

COLIN. No ... No one yet.

MRS SHAW. Honestly. If you'd have told us last night! I am pleased ... After all these years.

COLIN. Yep.

MRS SHAW. Going to take the plunge ... I thought you'd never get to it. (*She laughs*) ... Oh!

(SHAW *appears*).

I thought you'd gone to work or something.

SHAW. No, no. Just waking them lot upstairs.

MRS SHAW. We've just got some news to tell you ... Are you feeling all right?

SHAW. Yes. What news?

MRS SHAW. Nay. You've to be in a proper mood to hear it. (*To* COLIN) I told you he'd drunk too much last night.

SHAW. I am in a proper mood ... (*Looking at* COLIN.)

COLIN. I was telling my mother ... I might be getting married. Fairly soon.

MRS SHAW. Fairly soon ... (*To* COLIN.)

SHAW. Aye. Well. That's very good.
(*Pause.*)

MRS SHAW. Aren't you going to say more than that?

SHAW. Nay, well. I'm very pleased.

MRS SHAW. Well, if that's all you have to say.

SHAW. No. Well ... Congratulations, lad. (*Shakes his hand formally*) It's a grand thing, I can see that.

MRS SHAW. Well, you don't have to tell us ... Here ... there's your breakfast ... (*Pleasant.*)

SHAW. Nay ... I didn't sleep too well last night ... Nay, I'm pleased, Colin ... When are we going to see her?

COLIN. I was just saying ... I might bring her up. Or you could come down ...

SHAW. Aye ...
(ANDREW's *cheerful whistling off.*)

MRS SHAW. Wait till the others hear ... That'll wake them up. (*Laughs.*)
(ANDREW *comes in.*)

ANDREW. Morning. Morning. Morning. And a lovely day it is.

MRS SHAW. It is. He's right for once.

ANDREW. I am ... And how's my old mater this morning? Apple of my eye.

MRS SHAW. I'm very well, thank you. (ANDREW *kisses her cheek with a loud embrace.*)

ANDREW. Been dreaming about you, I have.

MRS SHAW. I hope something pleasant for a change.

ANDREW. Oh, very pleasant. Very. (*To* COLIN) And how are you, old chap, today?

COLIN. All right.

MRS SHAW. He's just given us some very wonderful news. That's how well he's feeling.

ANDREW. He's not ... Good God ... he can't be ... For one minute there I thought he might be pregnant.

MRS SHAW. He's getting married. Fairly soon. That's all he's got to say.

ANDREW. Oh ... Look at this. Dried up ... Tea cold. (*Examines the breakfast.*)

MRS SHAW. Is that all you've got to say?

ANDREW. Well done. Poor sod. Oh, dear. Whatever it is that's recommended.

MRS SHAW. Well, I must say.

SHAW. Nay, mother. Just leave them to it.

ANDREW. That's right. Settle it up amongst ourselves.

(MRS SHAW *starts to take the teapot to the kitchen.*)

No, no. It's hot enough. No, no. Really, I assure ... I was merely pulling your leg. And ... er ... (*To* COLIN) When's this happy event going to take place, Col?

COLIN. It hasn't been announced yet.

ANDREW. She hasn't started suing you yet?

COLIN. No: merely that it hasn't been announced.

ANDREW. I hope she's one of us, Col. I mean, not one of them ...

MRS SHAW. A dentist.

ANDREW. A dentist! By God. (*To* SHAW) I knew he'd marry a sadist. Formative experience: can't beat it. Every time ... this tastes very nice ... Good job you came up with the goods, Col. My mother was beginning to get worried. (*To* SHAW) Thought he might be one of those ... (*Quivers his hand.*)

MRS SHAW. I thought nothing of the kind.

ANDREW. Must have thought something ... I mean, all that time, you couldn't have thought nothing.

MRS SHAW (*reasonably*). I thought he was taking his time.

ANDREW. Taking his time. He's been through half a dozen motors cars while we've been waiting ... thought he'd given up the human race ... look well if he'd fathered a string of shooting brakes, or a line of two-tone limousines, as it is ... well done. Come up to scratch.

MRS SHAW. What did I tell you? Same as usual. (*To* COLIN.)

ANDREW (*to* MRS SHAW). What did you tell him?

MRS SHAW. Well, nothing, exactly. Except we might have expected something like that.

ANDREW. Oh, might you? I'm as predictable as that?

SHAW. Now look. Let's just have our breakfast ... I'll just give Steven another shout.

MRS SHAW. Nay, you don't have to defend him. He's always been old enough to look after himself.

ANDREW. I have. She's right. Ever since I was turned out I've been able to look after myself.

MRS SHAW. You weren't turned out.

ANDREW. No. No. Brought back into the fold, now. I remember. (*Embraces her*) Here's Steve, now, looking as bright as a Christmas penny ...

(STEVEN *has come in from the stairs*.)

MRS SHAW. Good morning, love. How are you?

STEVEN. Well ... Thanks.

ANDREW. Aren't you going to give your mother a birthday kiss? Forty-first year of marital bliss we're moving into.

MRS SHAW. He's got out of the bed the wrong side this morning.

ANDREW. I have. Same every day. Without exception.

(STEVEN *embraces* MRS SHAW.)

Well, then. That's that. Colin's got an announcement to make.

STEVEN. What's that?

ANDREW. Nothing calamitous. Don't worry ... Not for us at least, it isn't.

MRS SHAW. He's trying to say – I don't know whether you can tell – that Colin is going to get married.

STEVEN. Oh.

ANDREW. Galvanized him into action. Look.

STEVEN (to COLIN). Congratulations.

COLIN. Thanks.

MRS SHAW. Well, I don't know. What's got into you this morning?

ANDREW. I think it's the atmosphere up here ... Industrial pollution. It's noticeable the moment you step off that train.

SHAW (to ANDREW). Look ... what ... when ... ?

COLIN. We'll be going in a few minutes.

MRS SHAW. Oh, now. As quickly as that?

ANDREW. That's all right ... Important meetings. The destiny of the nation ... Steve and I can prop our feet up a little longer. Keep things ticking over.

COLIN. I thought you were coming back with me.

ANDREW. Well, I am. But I'm not leaving at this hour. Damn it all. I've only just got up. If you were an artist you'd understand these things.

COLIN (looking at his watch). Well, I'm going pretty soon. If you want a lift you better hurry.

ANDREW. The arrogance of the man. S'what comes with property and position. No, no ... I'll probably hitch one instead. Haven't done it, I must confess, for some considerable time, and it is some distance. Nevertheless, I think – speaking, of course, entirely as an artist – the insecurity might do me good.

COLIN. Yes ... well.

MRS SHAW. For me you can stay all day. You know that. We see so little of you ...

ANDREW. You're very kind. And we appreciate it, don't we, lads?

(*No answer.*)

MRS SHAW. Well, I don't know. You've all got up all right ... Next time we have one of these I'll see you don't drink as much, for one thing ... Aren't you going to have anything, Steve?

STEVEN. No ... I ... This tea is fine.

MRS SHAW. Well, if that's all you're eating, then, I can start clearing this away.

ANDREW. Yes. Yes. I think that might be in order.

(MRS SHAW *waits.*)

STEVEN. Oh ... Sorry, I'll give you a hand.

MRS SHAW. Thanks, love.

COLIN. Here ... I'll take that.

ANDREW (*to* COLIN). Give em a good wash will you, while you're at it. You never know, the experience might come in handy. A dentist ... (*to* SHAW) You know, I always thought that they were men.

(COLIN *and* STEVEN *clear the table into the kitchen.*)

SHAW. Well, I better be getting my work things out.

MRS SHAW. Work things! What on earth's the matter? You're not going to work for ... what? Ten hours.

SHAW. Aye ... Well ...

MRS SHAW. The way you're looking I think you ought to stay home another day. In bed. I've told you. Once you start, you just don't know how much you're drinking.

SHAW. Aye, well, I've played one night. I can't play another.

ANDREW. I think it'd be better, Dad, if you retired altogether.

SHAW. What?

ANDREW. My mother was saying before. It doesn't do anyone any good, this endless digging, digging, digging ... What're you trying to dig out anyway?

SHAW. What ... ?

COLIN (*reappearing*). Look ...

ANDREW. No, no. I was just asking. For his own good, Colin, as it were.

SHAW. I'm not trying to dig out anything.

ANDREW. No, no. I mean, you'd be silly if you were, wouldn't you? I mean, there's nothing down there, is there, but lumps of bloody coal.

SHAW (*to* MRS SHAW). Look ... I'll go up and get dressed.

ANDREW. You are dressed.

COLIN. It's time I was leaving ...

MRS SHAW. What on earth ... ?

ANDREW. The trouble is, Mother, you see ...

SHAW. That's enough!

ANDREW. We had an argument last night. After you'd gone to bed. One of the usual Shaw domestic tourneys: nothing to get excited about. You were probably too replenished to hear our little contretemps, but one or two people here, unless I'm severely mistaken, got very worked up indeed.

  (STEVEN *has come to stand in the door from the kitchen.*)

MRS SHAW. Oh. And what was all that about?

COLIN. ⎫ You needn't ...

SHAW. ⎭ It wasn't ...

ANDREW. Well, you'll be very pleased to hear, Ma ... (*Waits, looking round*) ... politics.

MRS SHAW. Well, I know he gets very worked up about that.

ANDREW. Oh, he does. I mean, I suppose, with all our years of experience, we ought to be ready for it. But no: stick a pig. We'll never change.

MRS SHAW. It's a good job I wasn't there ... I'd still have fallen asleep.

ANDREW. You would. You would. It's true. Nid-nod.

MRS SHAW. I would have thought, in any case, you were all on the same side. Your background, and the experience you've had ... (*She's finishing off the table, putting the cloth away, etc.*)

ANDREW. Oh, it's true. We are. It's just that Steven, unbeknown to us, as it were, had some very unusual opinions to express … I mean, that caught us unprepared.

MRS SHAW (*laughs*). Oh, and what opinions were those, then, Steve?

(*He stands in the doorway and shakes his head*)

Well, if you don't want me to know …

ANDREW. No, no. Come on, Steve. I mean, it's all over. We've settled, as it were, the issues out of hand … What opinions were they?

MRS SHAW. Nay, love. If you don't want me to hear, that's quite all right. I'm broad-minded enough, I think, for most things.

ANDREW. That's what she says.

STEVEN (*to* ANDREW. Look … I appreciated … what you said. Last night (*As* SHAW *begins to intervene:* 'Look … ') No, Dad … (*To* ANDREW) But judgments, in certain situations, come very easily to hand.

ANDREW. You've got to make a decision sometime, Steve.

STEVEN. I've made my decision.

ANDREW. Decision! Steve!

STEVEN. I've *made* my decision. You, of course, can ignore it. If you like … But actually, I've made it.

(ANDREW *gazes at him for a while.*

MRS SHAW *stands watching them, puzzled, smiling.*)

ANDREW. I too, then, have a choice?

STEVEN. Yes …

(ANDREW *weighs his hand, as if he holds the handle of a sword.*)

ANDREW. Vengeance … is mine, then.

STEVEN. Yes …

ANDREW. Saith the Lord.

STEVEN. I don't want you doing any damage here.

ANDREW. Here?

STEVEN. I don't want you doing any harm.

ANDREW. Harm.

> (*He looks slowly round the room, his gaze finally coming to rest on* MRS SHAW.
>
> *The others are rigid, silent: she still gazes at him, smiling, puzzled.*
>
> *He smiles back at her. Then:*)

ANDREW. Is it true ... your father was a breeder ...

MRS SHAW. A breeder?

ANDREW. Of livestock ... And the like?

MRS SHAW. Well, he had a few ...

SHAW. Look ... Here ...

ANDREW. I seem to remember ... Kept in little pens.

MRS SHAW. That's right ... (*Smiling.*)

ANDREW. Pigs ... I remember you telling us, often. Not dirty animals at all, unless their environment was allowed to become polluted.

MRS SHAW. Yes ... That's right.

ANDREW. Kept them very clean.

MRS SHAW. He did ... He looked after them very well.

ANDREW. Habit.

MRS SHAW. What?

ANDREW. I say. A habit ... cultivated by his daughter.

MRS SHAW. Well, I ... (*Looks to the others, smiling.*)

COLIN. Look ...

ANDREW. S'all right ... S'all right. S'all right ... No harm ... no harm ...

> (*To* COLIN). Would you mind?

COLIN. What ...

ANDREW. Warming up the engine ...

COLIN. What ... (STEVEN *gestures at him.*)

STEVEN. Go on, then, Col ... Go on.

MRS SHAW. Well ... I don't know ... I've always said we were a funny family.

> (COLIN, *a wild look round, then goes.*)

ANDREW. Funny. I think we are. By any standard. A family of comedians. Clowns. Excruciating tricks. Everything, for your amusement, Ma ...

MRS SHAW. Well, I'm not sure we're as good as that.

ANDREW. Oh, I think we are. Don't underrate us. Ask my dad. The strongest here ... Take all the weight. The lightest climb to the very top, and there ... take all the praise. Acknowledgment ... adulation ...

MRS SHAW. Well, drink's done *him* no harm at all.

ANDREW. The harm that I was done, was done a very long time ago indeed.

MRS SHAW. He's nearly as bad as he was last night.

ANDREW. I am bad. I am ...

STEVEN. Andy ...

ANDREW. Do you remember when I used to cry outside that door ... 'Let me in! Let me in!'

MRS SHAW. Oh, now ...

ANDREW. Why wasn't it ever opened? *Why?*

STEVEN. Andy ...

ANDREW. Why wasn't it ever opened, Steve?

STEVEN. *Andy* ...

ANDREW (*shouts*). Why wasn't it ever opened, Steve?

    (ANDREW *gazes at* STEVEN. *Then he goes slowly to* MRS SHAW.)

ANDREW (*to* MRS SHAW). Shall we dance?

MRS SHAW. Well, I ... (*Laughs as he puts out his arms*) Honestly, I don't know what we're coming to ...

ANDREW. Salvation. I can feel it in my bones.

    (ANDREW *has started dancing with* MRS SHAW *who is laughing, flushed.*)

MRS BURNETT (*popping in her head*). Well, then. All up. I thought I'd have to come round and ring a bell.

MRS SHAW. You've come just at the right moment, love, I think! (*Disengaging herself.*)

MRS BURNETT. Has he been to bed? Or is he on his way?

ANDREW. We're on our way. About to take our leave. The others, as you can see, are somewhat overwhelmed. Events have caught up with them so to speak. While I ... well, I'm afraid that I too have been overrun. Encapsulated. Caught well before my time ...

MRS BURNETT. Well, I don't know ...

MRS SHAW. Well, I don't either. It's some joke of theirs left over from last night.

MRS BURNETT. If you want a bit of fun you know what house to come to! (*Laughs.*)

REARDON (*appearing*). Hello. Hello. Hello. What's this? What's this? What's this? Signs of departure. Sounds of festivity and laughter ... Colin warming up his aeroplane outside ...

SHAW. Aye. Come in, lad. Come in.

ANDREW. Just leaving. About to take our leave.

REARDON. So I see ... So I see ...

STEVEN. Look. I'll just pop up.

MRS SHAW. All right, love ... I'm sorry you're going now, so soon. (*To* MRS BURNETT) They've all got work to go to ... except Andrew here, of course.

ANDREW. Always the sole exception ... Compassion. I can feel it in my bones.

REARDON. Men of the world. What a place they have to go to.

MRS BURNETT. They have. They have. You're right.

REARDON. Brimful of opportunity ... Round them on every side ... Wish I had my time over again, Harry.

SHAW. Aye.

REARDON. The journey to the stars! What a damn fine future lies before them.

SHAW. Aye.

COLIN (*coming in, wiping hands on a cloth*). Well, then. All set ... A car like that. You'd think you'd have no trouble ...

SHAW. Aye.

COLIN (*sees* ANDREW). Yes. Well, then ... If you're ready.

ANDREW. Steven is on his way. Packing his few things together.

COLIN. Right, then ... Well. I'm sorry it's been so short, Mother.

MRS SHAW. So am I, love. Maybe when you bring your ...

COLIN. Aye. Well. Tell them when I've gone, love.

MRS SHAW (*laughing*). Oh, all right, then ... And maybe when *he* retires we'll be able to arrange something better.

ANDREW. Aye. Let's hope so. Keep my eye open, Dad, I shall.

MRS SHAW. Well, goodbye, love. (*Embraces* COLIN) And I'm very pleased about you-know-what.

COLIN. Aye. Well. Goodbye, Mother ... 'Bye, Dad. (*Shakes* SHAW's *hand*.)

SHAW. Aye. Goodbye, lad ... And congratulations.

ANDREW. Look after them, Mr Reardon. They're very precious. Keep your eye on them, you know. (*To* MRS BURNETT) He kept an eye on me once, you know, when I was a little lad. Never looked back since then.

REARDON. Nay, I wouldn't claim any credit for that. (*Laughs*) I'll watch them.

ANDREW. Goodbye, then, Mother. Let's have a kiss.

(*They embrace.*)

MRS SHAW. Goodbye, love. And a bit less of that joking.

ANDREW. Aye. Aye. I promise that ... Goodbye, Dad ... Remember, now, when you're down that pit. Dig one out for me.

SHAW. Aye.

(ANDREW *has taken his father's hand.*)

ANDREW. Remember, now.

SHAW. Aye. I'll remember. (*Holds his hand a moment longer, gazing at him.*)

ANDREW. Right, then ... Best be off.

(STEVEN *has come on* ... ANDREW *turns away and he and* COLIN *start saying goodbye to* REARDON *and* MRS BURNETT.)

STEVEN. Goodbye, Mother.

MRS SHAW. Goodbye, love. And take care.

STEVEN. Aye. I will.

(*They embrace.*)

MRS SHAW. You'll remember, now?

STEVEN. Aye. I will ... 'Bye, Dad.

SHAW. 'Bye, lad. (*Takes his hand.*)

STEVEN. Here ... give you a kiss, an' all, shall I ...

(*Kisses his father's cheek, then embraces him. They're silent a moment.*)

ANDREW. Well, then. Off we get.

STEVEN. 'Bye, Mrs Burnett ... Keep your eye on them.

MRS BURNETT. I will, love. Don't you fret. (*Shakes his hand.*)

STEVEN. Mr Reardon ...

REARDON. Aye. Remember. Future of the nation in your hands ... (*They shake.*)

STEVEN. Aye ... I'll try.

MRS SHAW. And he's got four of his own to remind him.

(*They laugh.*)

COLIN. Right, then ...

STEVEN. After you.

COLIN. No, no. Youngest first. Always shall be.

STEVEN. Goodbye, then ...

SHAW. Goodbye, lad. Goodbye ... We'll see you off.

REARDON. Aye ...

(STEVEN *goes.*)

ANDREW (*to* COLIN). After you, old pal ... First time I've seen him without a shave.

(*They laugh.*)

COLIN. Aye ... Right. (*He goes.*)

SHAW (*to* MRS SHAW). Are you coming out, love?

MRS SHAW. No, no ... You go. I'll see them off from here.

REARDON. Aye. We'll give them a shove. They'll need it.

SHAW. Aye ... Come on. These city lads'll need a spot of muscle.

REARDON. Aye!

(*They go.*

Laughter and shouts off: 'Make way! Make way! ... Here he comes ... '

MRS SHAW *is left alone. She goes to the window, gazes out. Watches, moving back one of the curtains, slightly. She gets out a handkerchief, then wipes her eyes. Blows her nose.*

Shouts from outside: she puts her handkerchief down and waves. After a while the shouting dies.

Silent. She gazes out a moment longer, then lets the curtain fall. She straightens it, turns back to the room. Abstracted, she straightens a cushion, etc.

After a moment SHAW *comes back in, slow.*)

SHAW. Well, then ... that's that, eh?

MRS SHAW. Yes ...

SHAW. Did you enjoy it, love?

MRS SHAW. I did. Yes ... And you?

SHAW. Aye ... Aye.

MRS SHAW. They never change.

SHAW. Aye.

MRS SHAW. What was all that about, then?

SHAW. Nay, search me, love ... Now then. Where do you want me? Here. Look. Let me give you a start.

(*Goes to help her.*)

LIGHT SLOWLY FADES